D1760642

Violence

explained

COLLEGE LIF

BLACKBURN COLLEGE LIBRARY

REFERENCE COPY

NOT TO BE REMOVED FROM THE LIBRARY

Political analyses

Series editors: Bill Jones, Michael Clarke and Michael Moran

Brendan Evans and Andrew Taylor
From Salisbury to Major: continuity and change in Conservative politics

Michael Foley and John E. Owens
Congress and the presidency: institutional politics in a separated system

E. Franklin Dukes
Resolving public conflict: transforming community and governance

Stuart Croft
Strategies of arms control: a history and typology

Roland Axtmann
Liberal democracy into the twenty-first century: globalization, integration and the nation state

Violence explained

The sources of conflict, violence and crime and their provention

John W. Burton

Foreword by Vivienne Jabri

Manchester University Press
Manchester and New York

distributed exclusively in the USA by St Martin's Press

Copyright © John W. Burton 1997

Published by Manchester University Press
Oxford Road, Manchester M13 9NR, UK
and Room 400, 175 Fifth Avenue, New York, NY 10010, USA

Distributed exclusively in the USA
by St Martin's Press, Inc., 175 Fifth Avenue, New York,
NY 10010, USA

British Library Cataloguing-in-Publication Data
A catalogue record for this book is available from the British Library

Library of Congress Cataloging-in-Publication Data applied for

ISBN   0 7190 5047 2   *hardback*
ISBN   0 7190 5048 0   *paperback*

First published 1997

01 00 99 98 97   10 9 8 7 6 5 4 3 2 1

BLACKBURN COLLEGE
LIBRARY
Acc. No. *BC 94423*
Class No. HSC 303.6 BUR
Date *10/10/02*

Printed in Great Britain by
Biddles Ltd, Guildford and King's Lynn

To parents, teachers, managers, lawyers,
diplomats and politicians

Contents

Series editor's foreword

The Politics Today series has been running successfully since the late 1970s, aimed mainly at an undergraduate audience. After over a decade in which a dozen or more titles have been produced, some of which have run to multiple editions, Manchester University Press thought it time to launch a new politics series, aimed at a different audience and a different need.

The Political Analyses series is prompted by the relative dearth of research-based political science series, which persists despite the fecund source of publication ideas provided by current political developments.

In the United Kingdom we observe, for example: the rapid evolution of Labour politics as the party seeks to find a reliable electoral base; the continuing development of the post-Thatcher Conservative Party; the growth of pressure group activity and lobbying in modern British politics; and the irresistible moves towards constitutional reform of an arguably outdated state.

Elsewhere, there are even more themes upon which to draw, for example: the ending of the Thatcher–Reagan axis; the parallel collapse of communism in Europe and Russia; and the gradual retreat of socialism from the former heartlands in Western Europe.

This series will seek to explore some of these new ideas to a depth beyond the scope of the Politics Today series – whilst maintaining a similar direct and accessible style – and to serve an audience of academics, practitioners and the well-informed reader as well as undergraduates. The series has three editors: Bill Jones and Michael Moran, who will concentrate on domestic UK topics, and Michael Clarke, who will attend to international issues.

Bill Jones

Foreword

John W. Burton is one of the most important and controversial founders of Conflict Studies as a distinct area of social and political thought. This book is an updated version of his *Deviance, Terrorism and War*, published in 1979. It is also a restatement of a position which has since been elaborated and commented upon. Burton's influence in the field remains unparalleled in its radicalism and its capacity to generate intellectual debate. This is also a work of consolidation; one which places emphasis on Burton's innovative thoughts on conflict resolution and renders these in a style that is accessible to a non-academic or policy-oriented audience.

The value of *Violence Explained* lies in its capacity to question the prevailing order, to highlight salient problems that beset societies, both domestic and international, and to suggest methods through which we as a global society may begin to handle these. There is no false modesty about John Burton or his corpus. In these pages he points to the complexity of the problem of violence while at the same time underpinning an unflinching commitment to what he calls 'problem-solving' as a method of resolving conflicts which escalate towards violence. Where *Deviance, Terrorism and War* was aimed at a largely sceptical academic audience, one located within the 'realist' led discipline of International Relations, this book aims for a wider public, one which is aware of and contains the institutions which Burton sees as being implicated in the violent conflicts we see around us.

Burton's original contributions to the field of Conflict Studies started in the 1960s with the publication of *Conflict and Communication*, which used insights from cognitive psychology to establish a theoretical base for an innovative approach to conflict resolution at the international level. The intellectual backdrop was set in place and the Centre for the Analysis of Conflict (CAC) came into being as an institutional forum dedicated to the study of conflict and its resolution. For a former diplomat working within an academic setting, the establishment of such a forum would allow him and scholars from a number of disciplines to combine a theoretical interest in the study of conflict with the practical experience of facilitating the resolution of conflicts as non-official intermediaries. The radical statement of the project was its challenge to the positivist dualism between theory and practice and, more controversially for a discipline then dominated by the ideals of positivism, it recognized the praxiological potentialities of the discourses around human behaviour which were then prevalent. Far from a stress on remaining on the outside of the actual world studied, Burton called for direct involvement, not, as is the strategist's purview, on the theme of how to win a war, but precisely in the name of peace and the resolution of conflict. The historical context which surrounded these activities – the Cold War, decolonization, and wars of secession – seemed to be a world apart from the tranquil surroundings of University College, London, where the CAC was based, and the seminar rooms where Burton's ideas took shape and were tested out on colleagues such as Michael Banks, John Groom, Chris Mitchell, Tony de Reuk and Bram Oppenheim, among others. The UK-based CAC became involved in the Cyprus conflict and the dispute between Indonesia, Malaysia and Singapore. Colleagues from the United States, including Herb Kelman, Chad Alger and Robert North, were also included in conflict resolution exercises.

In these early days of the CAC, Burton and his colleagues were also gradually introducing a radically new discourse in International Relations as a discipline. The state and inter-state system were no longer considered the only possible arenas of investigation and power was not the all-pervading independent variable. The individual as a behaving entity was brought into the discipline and with the individual a widening of its discursive boundaries to incorporate a multidisciplinary approach to the study of such issues as identity, nationalism, poverty and violence. What Burton later called the 'world society' approach was, for Michael Banks, one of the challenging paradigms to realism, where the discursive stress on power was replaced by a focus on interactive communication and interdependence. There was no idealism here, but a self-reflexive understanding that the discourses of the discipline were implicated in the construction of the world and, more saliently, that theoretical understanding did not preclude the possibility of active engagement.

It is this element of active engagement which has had most influence in the field of Conflict Studies and which has placed Burton at the heart of debates around the question of responses to conflict. Where, traditionally, great faith was invested in official mediation and the process of diplomacy as a means for the settlement of conflict, Burton introduced to the discipline of International Relations the idea that scholarship always had praxiological implications and that a radically questioning project implied innovation not only in our theoretical frameworks but in modes of response to conflicts. The innovation here was not so much the non-official character of intervention – Adam Curle and other Quaker mediators had an already existing established tradition in non-official mediation – but a self-conscious integration of theory and practice. It is this element of Burton's work which has attracted what is at times referred to as a 'second generation' of conflict resolutionists, younger scholars taught by Burton and his colleagues and engaged practically in conflict resolution projects.

Burton's work has therefore been both influential and inspiring. Like all works which have an impact, it has also created controversy and disagreement. As a member of the second generation and whose interest in conflict was instilled by Burton, I certainly feel a sense of privilege in being asked to write this foreword. This is especially so as Burton knows my own work on violent conflict and is fully aware of the fact that I espouse a radically different theoretical approach to the study of conflict and peace. What remains for this foreword is for me to point to the controversies which Burton's work has generated after providing a sketch of what is on offer in this book.

Burton's framework is based on a dualism defined as the 'power frame' and the 'problem-solving frame'. The latter is grounded in the view that human beings have certain ontological needs which are common across cultures and other socially constructed boundaries. These are defined as drives, the violation of which leads to conflict and crime, while the satisfaction of which, through problem-solving processes, prevents violence. This seemingly simple formula leads Burton to suggest that such diverse problems as family breakdown, industrial strife, ethnic conflict and international conflict have the same source (human needs) and may be amenable to 'resolution' through the same process ('problem-solving'). For Burton, such needs as identity, recognition and security are not in themselves sources of conflict, but only become so as they are suppressed by societal institutions. Echoing Galtung's concept of structural violence, Burton ascribes fault to structural continuities which constrain human development. Furthermore, where such constraint may aim at the imposition of order and stability, it achieves precisely the opposite, in that the fulfilment of needs such as identity will be pursued by human agents regardless of consequences.

I will summarize two critiques of Burton's thought which in my view are worth considering. One of the primary critiques of Burton's work relates to his definition of needs as acultural attributes, the violation of which is a source of conflict. Once conflict is seen as a social phenomenon, however, the complex arena of society and its discursive and institutional structures must be taken into account if we are to understand the processes through which the individual relates to community, group or state. Social identity is a complex site of contestation for a constantly fragmenting and shifting subjectivity. Identity is always constructed and recursive at one and the same time. It emerges from the symbolic realm and from the normative and institutional continuities which constitute society, but every expression of identity is itself implicated in the reproduction of such continuities. The human being is no mere collection of drives, therefore, but is always engaged and always implicated in the reproduction of the institutions which Burton implicates in the emergence of violent conflict and crime. Moreover, the individual has a reflexive capacity which enables her or him to judge behaviours and circumstances and to express this in discursive, interactive and interpretive mode. To suggest that the individual is driven by needs, the violation of which could lead to violent conflict, is also to remove the moral agency from the individual, that capacity for the judgement of actions not only in terms of self-interest but of the continuation of norms which sustain community and solidarity.

Burton uses the vehicle of human needs to explain violence across different levels of social interaction. The difficulty associated with this holistic approach is that the individual exists within differing systems of enablement and constraint which cannot be equated across societal structures. The family structure, for instance, imposes constraint or enables the individual differently from class structure, the legal framework within society, the state or international society. The individual is a situated entity, and this situatedness defines the social formations which are both a product of individual behaviour and constitutive of an individual's definition of self.

The second point of critique relates to Burton's ideas on conflict resolution and his commitment to a process which has come to be known as problem-solving. It is specifically Burton's dualism between power and problem-solving, or settlement and resolution of conflict, which has been the subject of challenge. In seeking to deny power a place in the resolution of conflict, Burton wishes to stress that outcomes based on coercion cannot be a basis for long-lasting and self-reinforcing resolution. Where traditional modes of negotiation and mediation may achieve outcomes to interest-based conflicts, such techniques must remain inadequate in the face of needs-based conflicts such as those centred around identity or security. For these require a process of facilitated interaction where the parties are allowed to explore mutual needs and the obstacles to open communication.

The conflict resolution process cannot, however, be reduced to dualism between power and problem-solving as this would seem to negate the possibility that these two modes of intervention may be effective at different points during the lifecycle of a conflict. This statement is more a recognition of the limitations of the problem-solving mode of conflict resolution than its wholesale rejection. It argues that rather than conceptualizing the third-party process in the dichotomous terms advocated by Burton, we could suggest that different modes of intervention come to define a whole process of peacemaking which is interactive and complementary. Problem-solving is only one of these processes, and may only be possible once violence is terminated and negotiation established as a form of communication. The point is that such complex situations as Bosnia or the Israeli-Palestinian conflict present such cases of emergency that problem-solving can only be considered a distant possibility.

Mediation based on power, in other words, sets the stage, brings the intransigent to the table, and enables ultimate problem-solving. If this is so in domestic and international conflicts, the institutionalization of problem-solving as a form of dispute resolution connected to the courts at the societal level is merely a vindication of the view that while problem-solving is an enabling process, it in turn must be enabled.

Despite the controversies and objections surrounding Burton's ideas, there is a widespread recognition of his role in introducing problem-solving as a conflict resolution process to theorists and practitioners alike. Always himself the practitioner, Burton has sought to establish an ethic of active engagement in the name of sustainable peace.

What must finally be said, however, is that this book is a powerful statement in support of innovation in the means we use to handle humanity's 'deadly quarrels'. While we in the specialized fields of Conflict Studies and International Relations may have our intellectual disagreements around the causes of conflict and the methods we advocate for the resolution of conflict, the element which we share is a self-reflexive awareness of the place of understanding in contributing to the amelioration of the human condition.

Vivienne Jabri
University of Kent

Preface

Burton's intention

This book is about the insecurities and anxieties that all members of societies experience as conflict, violence and crime invade daily living. It is dedicated to parents, teachers, managers, lawyers and politicians, all of whom have a role to play in combatting violence, but in order to do so they require the support and understanding of the wider community. Only by seeking to explain violence can we begin to deduce means of *proventing** it.

A research interest in the sources of conflict, and its resolution, developed in the 1960s, with a focus on particular conflict situations within and between nations. The area of interest soon shifted to specific industrial and social conflicts. Those applying their theories then realized that resolving one problem did not prevent others occurring, and sought to deduce the generic sources of such aggressive behaviours and means of their prevention. In the 1980s a general theory emerged which could be applied at all social levels and in all cultures. Its focus was the way in which social and economic structures frustrate basic human needs, such as the needs for recognition and identity, leading to protest and frustration responses. This explanation of conflict provided the basis of policies to provent conflict, violence and anti-social behaviours generally. Rather than coercive compliance measures, there could be analytical problem-solving processes that reveal the sources of problems in relationships, leading to possible reconciliation.

This book seeks to go one step further and to examine the family and various public institutions, to see what they would look like if there were a *problem-solving approach* rather than an *adversarial power approach* in domestic, national and international relationships, and to stimulate thinking on how change can be achieved.

---

* Provention: The term *prevention* has the connotation of containment. The term *provention* has been introduced to signify taking steps to remove sources of conflict, and more positively to promote conditions in which collaborative and valued relationships control behaviours.

Acknowledgements

Apart from the many authors to whom references have been made, I hesitate to make personal acknowledgements as no listing could include all those relatives, friends, colleagues and students with whom I have had conversations and from whom I have gained insights into the complex social problems of conflict and violence which are now of widespread concern. They will recognize ideas and recall conversations. They will not necessarily wholly agree with my interpretations. Special thanks are due, however, to Racheal and Kate Krinks, for their helpful younger generation comments; also to Dr Doug Cocks, an ecologist, and to Betty Nathan, both themselves authors, who have made a great number of insightful editorial and substantive suggestions. It was kind of Dr Vivienne Jabri to write a Foreword.

Part One

The human dimension

In any analysis of conflict, violence and crime there must be a consideration of human nature and of the way in which the social environment determines behaviour. Part One of this book is concerned with the human dimension. Members of the human race have shared physical characteristics and needs, such as for food and shelter. Less obvious, and frequently ignored, are shared needs for social recognition as individuals and as members of identity groups within a society. Denial of physical needs can be a source of conflict. The denial of psychological and social needs is probably a far more important cause of conflict. The pursuit of ethnic identity, for example, is sometimes at the expense of life itself. In industry the treatment of workers as robots or as persons may be as important an issue as wage levels.

We are not yet fully aware of the precise nature of human needs. The focus of Part One is, therefore, the *person* rather than *people* generally, and different but predictable patterns of behaviour – different *behaviours* – in different circumstances.

Part One, therefore, supplies the frame in which, in subsequent Parts, required changes in institutions are explored and means of change suggested. Chapter 1 outlines this approach to the analysis of conflict, violence and crime, and given this approach, in Chapter 2 the problem area is described. In Chapter 3 the key social problem of compliance is explored. This leads, in Chapter 4, to a reconsideration of basic human needs. In Chapter 5 there is a consideration of the principles which, accordingly, must be followed in decision-making if violence and crime are to be avoided.

1

The approach

The world is today in a situation of crisis – political, social and environmental. Political-social-economic systems are not being adjusted to human aspirations and needs, nor are the controls being introduced which are required by population increases and environmental deterioration.

This is not because of any lack of knowledge about the existence of serious political, social, population and resource problems and environmental damage. There has been a spate of books deploring emerging conditions, each dealing with a specific subject. Examples include Reich[1] on the global corporate economy and its effects on cultures and employment, Chomsky[2] and Kwitny[3] on US destruction of democracies in Central and Latin America, Schlesinger[4] and West[5] on deteriorating racial relationships in the United States, Postman[6] on the consequences of the dominance of technology in education at the expense of thinking and conceptualizing, and Brown and Singer[7] on the alarming deterioration in global environmental conditions. All deplore trends in their areas of special interest and give warnings about the future if these continue. Few come up with more than warnings, implying a depressing acceptance of the inevitable.

It is widely believed that there are points of no return in dealing with both human and environmental problems. Yet, with the exception of token aid measures to relieve suffering, the persistent response to conflict, violence and anti-social behaviours, national and international, has been to try to contain them by punishment and by deterrent strategies. Even though it has for a long time been clear that this tactic fails, little attention has been given to the sources of these behaviours and to appropriate means of avoiding their occurrence. Given failure, we have no option but to come up with an explanatory frame within which to analyse problems of conflict, violence and crime, and from which we can deduce appropriate structures and policies.

To help to avoid divisive subjectivity it is desirable first to set out the principles on which an analysis may be based. This is best begun by articulating an ideal or utopia that provides the direction or goal for the analysis. Sir

Thomas More invented the term utopia ('no place') in 1516 when describing his perfect but impossible island society. It served as a basis for his analysis of contemporary society. Using the same process, and having established general utopian principles, which should be reasonably uncontentious, consideration can then be given to practical proposals and how they may be implemented.

In his review of utopias Lewis Mumford observes that 'In negative form, the utopian ideal of total control from above, absolute obedience below, never entirely passed out of existence.'[8] The ideal was a city which operated as a machine, capable of making war and building the palaces and temples of elites in an orderly way. Frye observed in the same text: 'To Hobbes, a contemporary of the Puritan Revolution, the most important social principle was the maintenance of the *de facto* power ... To Locke, a contemporary of the Whig Revolution, the most important social principle was the relation of *de facto* power to legitimate or *de facto* authority.'[9] For all utopians, the machine required the powerful leader, his public servants and police, an army and, of course, those who were required to provide the necessary labour. Utopias were more efficient machines than was possible in practice, not different ones. Essentially, they were pictures of more effective ways by which power elites could secure the compliance of an underclass to the social norms established by the elite.

Recognize some key features? Policies in developed and developing countries, in democratic and dictatorial systems, are based on compliance systems. While communities disagree over the reasons for conflicts, violence and crime, and, therefore, how they are to be tackled, there is still a widely shared utopian belief that conformity with norms as they exist must be enforced.

There are some who believe that the source of conflict, violence and crime is personal and group irresponsibility, particularly the lack of social conscience. In this view, as was evident in the 'Contract with America' in the United States in 1994–95 and in the debates in the Congress over a Crime Bill, the appropriate policies include less supportive intervention by governments to help non-achievers, and greater freedom from government so that market incentives will encourage achievers and self-interested conformity. The social 'net' provided by government would include police, gaols and deterrent strategies rather than welfare payments.

There are, on the other hand, others who believe that conflict, violence and crime are due to social and structural problems, such as poverty, long-term unemployment and, at the international level, inappropriate boundaries between nations, which provoke anti-social behaviours. They believe that the appropriate policies are, for example, more welfare support, peace-keeping forces and foreign aid programmes.

These seemingly different approaches of separate political ideologies are not fundamentally different. Neither deals with root causes, both focusing on

This is topical

attitudes or social conditions current at the time in their societies and cultures. Both seek personal and group compliance with prevailing institutional and social norms, one by direct compliance measures, the other by first using persuasion and an appeal to moral conscience while keeping enforced compliance and punishment in reserve.

In getting down to sources it is not necessary to enter this debate. Both viewpoints may be valid. In recent years it has been recognized that 'A socially defined utopia loses its truth if it does not at the same time fulfill the person, just as the individually defined utopia loses its truth if it does not at the same time bring fulfillment to society.'[10]

If we are to tackle serious political-social problems we must start with a frame in which traditional assumptions give way to ones that reflect far more the human elements in social relations and the shared purposes of social organizations. For purposes of analysis we must invent our own utopia, one that takes into account the nature of those who must comply, and the nature of the norms and institutions with which there must be compliance.

While all utopias, all political philosophies, have assumed compliance, by force or by persuasion, to be the foundation of civilized societies and their organizations, it would seem that it is the compliance process itself which is at the core of anti-social responses to social norms. Whether it be the child in rebellion within the family, the unemployed teenager looking for an identity in a street gang, the seemingly deprived seeking to satisfy some need by theft, the routine worker on strike in industry, the ethnic minority within a society struggling for equality through autonomy, or the aggressive nation within the world society, the behaviour is the same: an unwillingness, and perhaps an inability, to comply with imposed prevailing norms and, therefore, rebellion against compliance constraints.

It is reliance on enforced or induced compliance that has to be addressed. The evidence is clear: conflict, violence and crime are on a scale that must call into question all of our traditional beliefs and assumptions. The compliance one is basic. We cannot assume any longer that it is acceptable to people that there are those who have the right, because of their power, to determine the rules and to expect obedience, and others who have an obligation to obey. When we attribute the problem of non-compliance behaviour to compliance-seeking institutions, this highlights the need for some specific changes in decision-making processes, and these go a long way towards addressing our problems. Acceptable institutional options have to be found. Hence the search for a human utopia comprising institutions in which concurrence and consent rather than compliance are the cement of relationships.[11]

This book seeks, first, to adopt a holistic approach, searching for the common sources of the seemingly separate problem areas of domestic and international conflict, violence and crime. Each relates to the others and specialization does not suggest remedies. Furthermore, conflict, violence and crime relate to unemployment and inequalities, these relate to educational opportunities and to health services, these are progressively limited by population increases and resource depletion, which relate to system failures in controlling exploitation of resources, which relate to pollution and environmental damage, and so on. Treating some specific problems separately accentuates others: financial policies designed to curb inflation lead to unemployment, the promotion of investment leads to inequalities, and these lead to social problems, etc.

Second, this book directs attention to the reasons why human evolution has taken its destructive course, and considers, not new systems or radical change, but mechanisms for continuing change in institutions and policies as a means of avoiding and resolving problems.

Notes

1 R. Reich, *The Work of Nations* (New York, Vintage Press, 1992).
2 N. Chomsky, *Year 501: The Conquest Continues* (Boston, South End Press, 1993). See also *Deterring Democracy* (New York, Hill and Wang, 1991).
3 J. Kwitny, *Endless Enemies: The Making of an Unfriendly World* (New York, Congdon and Weed, 1984).
4 A. M. Schlesinger, *The Disuniting of America: Reflections on a Multicultural Society* (New York, Norton and Co., 1992).
5 C. West, *Race Matters* (Boston, Beacon Press, 1993).
6 N. Postman, *Technopoly: The Surrender of Culture to Technology* (New York, Vintage Press, 1993).
7 B. Brown and P. Singer, *The Greens* (Melbourne, The Text Publishing Co., 1996).
8 L. Mumford, 'Utopia. The City and the Machine', in F. E. Manuel, ed., *Utopias and Utopian Thought* (London, Souvenir Press, 1973).
9 N. Frye, 'Varieties of Literary Utopias', in Manuel, ed., *Utopias and Utopian Thought*.
10 P. Tillich, 'Critique and Justification of Utopia', in Manuel, ed., *Utopias and Utopian Thought*.
11 Because of these problems there is a great deal of confusion in the use of terms: for example, the difference between consent and compliance. See J. Burton, *Conflict Resolution: Its Language and Processes* (Lanham MD, Scarecrow Press, 1996).

2

The problem area

Increasing insecurity

The human race has evolved into a large number of different societies, many of which have, thanks to an ever-widening political participation, become increasingly democratic and just. In recent years material living standards have improved greatly in many communities, thanks largely to technological achievements. Material living standards are, however, only part of the quality of life. Gains from technology are of decreasing importance when accompanied by a growing sense of physical and social insecurity. Indeed, improved quality of life is increasingly being sought after by even the more materially wealthy in societies, frequently despite great personal inconvenience.

In the United States the basic crime rate – property damage and violent crimes per 100,000 people – was 190 in 1960, 400 in 1970, and about 600 in the 1990s.[1] These are nationally averaged figures: the rates are far higher in certain localities. Behind these figures is the evolution of two Americas, the 'haves' and the 'have-nots'. The gap between the two Americas has become wider and wider in recent years. It will increase further as the global economy gives businesses increasing opportunities for routine work to be performed offshore. The United States is little different in this respect from other developed, largely Anglo-Saxon societies, such as Great Britain, Australia and Canada, which are all moving in the same direction. Many less developed countries have their own special problems of conflict and violence, and sometimes a decreasing quality of life despite technological benefits: for example the ex-colonial state of Sri Lanka and many African states, and also China and the tremendous region of the former Soviet Union.

A new era?

These symptoms of organizational failure have been a continuing part of history, but they seem now to be more than offsetting accompanying developmental benefits. In the past the means of violence were limited, and those that existed were not widely available. Behaviours were, consequently, more subject to control by authorities. Coerced compliance was to a large degree a reality. However, fuelled by developments in communications and the availability of modern weapons, violent behaviour is now universal. Street gangs are beyond police control. Ethnic minorities can break up multinational countries. Small countries can defeat the greatest of military powers. Effective defiance of authorities, national and international, is now widespread. Consequently, the kind of imbalance between, on the one hand, the gains from technological development and, on the other, decreases in personal security, is now part of social life. Despite this, in the absence of some acceptable option, there still remains a resistance to any fundamental change in political and economic structures or social policies.

The emerging defiance of authority is not the wave of conflict with authorities which in the past led to revolutions and changes in governments. It is a day-to-day defiance of authorities by small numbers of people acting alone or in small groups. It occurs in most societies and at all social levels, including the international, despite increased police and military operations. (We will continually be associating domestic conflicts, at all social levels, with international conflicts as though they are all one phenomenon. The reader, accustomed to domestic and international being treated as separate situations, even separate academic disciplines, may find this disturbing, but the reasons for such a holistic approach will become clear.) Such defiance is a recent phenomenon, a turning point in social evolution. While it is assisted by the availability of modern weapons and communication technologies, it is characterized by the emergence of human behaviours, once widely suppressed, as a force greater than that of the power of authorities. As will become clear, it is a challenge to traditional coercive compliance structures, and as such a challenge to traditional social systems and political philosophies.

Defensive responses

In these circumstances the majority of members of affluent societies are caught between a sense of insecurity in the present and a fear for their material future if political and institutional change is contemplated to deal with the sources of their insecurity. As a consequence, the dysfunctional struggle to preserve the *status quo* by preventive means increases: more police, more gaols, more forces; and to pay for this, less aid for development, less support to public education and important services, leading to even greater inequalities and more alienation and conflict.

In an increasing number of developing countries there are, in addition to such community problems, famines and starvation caused by human agency, ethnic communities in conflict because of inappropriate post-colonial boundaries, and wars between ambitious leaders. Even so, there is a self-defeating resistance to system change, frequently backed by interested foreign powers.

Widespread in this crisis stage is, therefore, a frustrated acceptance of what is the only known policy option: more authoritarian containment, official violence to quell violence. Both the individual and community reaction is to seize whatever material and security benefits might be available. Societies are moving away from trends towards greater equality and justice which are associated with democracy and which for a short time dominated welfare policies in developed countries after the First World War. They are breaking up once again into separate communities in which are available vastly different degrees of physical security, of education, of health, of job opportunities and of resources.

Similarly at the international level powerful nations try to impose trading restrictions on others to suit their needs. 'Human rights' arguments are used to justify continuing trade restrictions on the imports of goods from countries with cheap labour – despite 'human rights' abuses in the countries imposing the restrictions. The competitive market system, dominated by the more powerful, thus further degrades relationships, despite possibilities of mutual economic advantage that could help to promote human rights. There is little long-term costing of policies as they evolve.

When change in domestic institutions or the international system does take place it is likely to be, as in the past, a change that reflects short-term interests and desperation. In the absence of a well-defined and acceptable option, change is likely to be toward yet another poorly-thought-through expedient which ignores causes and is, again, based on power.

Human behaviour versus systems

Divisions in societies extend beyond the workplace and social relations because they lead to a sense of alienation and a questioning of the acceptability of democracy as traditionally conceptualized. An emergence of a 'third world' in 'first world' countries gives rise to a sense of exclusion from the political system, and from decision-making processes in particular. As US Labor Secretary Robert Reich said in 1994, 'A society divided between the haves and the have-nots or the well educated and the poorly educated cannot be a stable society over time.'[2] Third world communities are characterized by widespread personal violence amongst their own members as anger is transferred, a violence that in due course spills over into more affluent regions.

Majority government democracies frequently prevail in countries in which there are alienated ethnic minorities. These are the 'unrepresented peoples' within states. Such minorities seek to achieve autonomies, as did colonial peoples after the Second World War. They can now do this with the use of modern weapons. Sovereign states, which are the units of the United Nations, together resist such movements towards secession.

The disruption that confronts national authorities reflects the 'power' of alienated members of societies – always in the past regarded as the powerless – seeking to pursue their own needs and to find places in society. This was acknowledged in 1988 in the title of a book, edited by Roger Coate and Jerel Rosati, *The Power of Human Needs*.[3] As a potential power it has always been present, but in changed political and technological conditions it is now erupting. Empirical evidence suggests that a paramount need being satisfied by the violent is the need for recognition as an individual or group.

Individuals in society have always employed whatever means are currently available to them to attain recognition and identity. These means include the now widespread frustration responses of young people who have no ordinary means of attaining a role in society. Typical responses include leaving home and school, joining street gangs, and enacting roles of violence at community and ethnic levels that attract attention and provide some individual recognition. Membership of a street gang and carrying a gun, where one is available as in the United States, is a practical solution to a lack of personal identity and to social alienation. More constructively, in modern societies such means frequently include forming and joining separate ethnic and religious organizations, trade unions and political parties which give support to those who find that mainstream institutions and social norms do not advance their important identity goals. But continued frustration and protest activities by such groups can lead to authoritative resistance and to violence.

Whatever may be the precise nature of this power of human needs – and attempts will later be made to identify it – societies are faced with the question whether authorities can any longer require individuals to adjust to existing institutions and traditional norms, or whether institutions and norms, traditionally oriented towards interests in production, must now be adjusted to human requirements.

Ignoring this question, brushing it aside on the grounds that problems of violence are merely passing problems due to economic recession or to some temporary set of conditions, or due perhaps to a lack by some of social conscience, ensures a worsening crisis. While this basic question is ignored, more and more containment and suppression by authorities are required. More and more containment leads to even wider protest and to the escalation of violence. What civilizations are experiencing is a general condition: incompatibilities between systems as they have evolved, on the one hand, and human drives, on the other. Specific problems, such as family violence, aggressive street gangs, ethnic conflict, secession movements and others, are merely symptoms of this underlying condition.

In so far as specific problems are being tackled by authorities as though they were separate problems, there can be no lasting cures for any of them. Indeed, the attempted 'cure' of any one, such as containment of violence by coercion and punishment, or treatment of ethnic conflict as though it were due merely to personal xenophobia, are likely, not only to be self-defeating, but also to stimulate other anti-social behaviour that will be no less intractable. For example, attempting to curb crime by more prisons and at the expense of professional interventions at the community level, leads to prisons becoming a source of further alienation and anger, and a training ground for further revenge crime. At another level, seeking to preserve boundaries which divide language and ethnic communities, as is the case in Africa, or to preserve sovereignty in the face of secession movements, as has been the case for so long in Cyprus and Sri Lanka, must lead to continuing social unrest and conflict.

In short, the question being posed in this book is, are dissidents abnormal, anti-social types of people, and, as a small minority, are they to be contained, or perhaps eliminated, as has been assumed in traditional thinking? Or is there some causal human drive which societies in the past have usually been able to suppress, but which now, in changed circumstances, has to be accommodated? Are changed circumstances, particularly the availability of technologies of violence, now forcing a recognition that there is a power within societies which is potentially far greater than the coercive power of the state and of any international organization comprising states?

Ideological approaches

In the past societies have tended, in the absence of adequate knowledge or an ability to prevent or to resolve problems, to retreat into ideological, religious or other reflexive positions, backed by police or military support. There being no consensus agreement for such positions, these expediency reactions have led to the further evolution of adversarial institutions and intense political confrontations, but rarely to constructive solutions.

In developed countries those in need have sought changes in societies through government interventions to improve living conditions. The economically successful and powerful, on the other hand, having little confidence in bureaucratic wisdom, have sought more freedom for the market, with interventions to promote private initiatives and investments. Both have become increasingly interest-oriented. The constituencies of both are now universally anxious about their futures, but find it impossible to move from an ideological and, therefore, confrontational stance, in tackling their shared problems.

Even if opposing capital and labour factions could resolve their problems, this would not deal with the problem facing the 20 per cent or so of the population of a developed economy, comprising the unemployed and youth seeking a role, minorities and others experiencing alienation. (The arbitrary 20 per cent notion will be used extensively in later chapters, although it should be borne in mind that in many cases populations which experience alienation may be far greater, especially in ethnically divided and underdeveloped countries. The 20 per cent figure will be used as short hand to characterize the alienation problem as distinct from the traditional capital versus labour problem.) Nor would resolving the domestic capital–labour problems deal with international problems of exploitation and poverty and associated ethnicity and leadership rivalries.

The industrial relations problem is important in itself. But while historically the market system might be a major contributor to these wider social problems, it is not in a position to deal with them. There is here a critical role for authorities, complicated by middle and upper-class resistance to many forms of intervention, especially those that might seem to reduce returns on capital without commensurate benefits.

Within the traditional we–they confrontational frame there have been many system changes in the past, for example in eighteenth-century France, Czarist Russia in the early twentieth century, and, more recently, in the former Soviet Union, to mention a few. In each case change was a desperate response to unacceptable circumstances. But that change was not based on a clear explanation of past failure, and it did not address source problems. Communism was a planned and fundamental change from capitalism, but in practice it turned out to be no less elitist. Compliance was through coercion by a small elite. It failed to take into account human considerations such as the need for a sense of participation in decision-making and the need for personal incentives at the workplace. It relied unrealistically on the assumption that a shared social goal would provide the necessary individual initiatives and incentives. Capitalism has taken many forms in many different circumstances. It has provided incentives, but when uncontrolled these have threatened the wider social and longer-term interests of all. Neither 'ism' has offered a participatory decision-making system, so necessary if human needs are to be met, and neither has been able to define the intervention role of authorities. Now we have a global society in which all authorities, regardless of the particular political or economic system in which they operate, are caught between the pressures of vested interests and those of basic human needs, and are unable to prevent the consequent alienation that is disrupting their societies.

An ideologically neutral approach

The argument of this book is, essentially, that the problems facing civilizations stem, not so much from their existing political and social systems, but how these are managed over time, including managed change as seems to be required. All systems have their faults in addition to their strengths. One focus of this analysis is on the decision-making failures of all societies, of which ideological rivalries and adversarial political processes are symptoms. More constructively, there is also a focus on means of resolving serious social problems by specific collaborative and problem-solving processes which involve all sections of societies.

12

But it goes further than this. The practice of an ideal collaborative problem-solving process is only a beginning. It is the *provention* of problems occurring that is required. In particular the provention of conflicts is required, especially in modern conditions in which high levels of violence are possible. But provention implies an accurate assessment and prediction of behaviours and of future local and global circumstances. This is rarely possible. No person or group, no parent, no political leader or party, no manager of industry, knows the answers to all the problems which they encounter, nor can they predict problems which they might face in the future. Problem-solving has to be, therefore, not only a collaborative effort, but an ongoing process so that adjustments to institutions and policies can take place in a continuing way as systems evolve, as conditions change, and as experience and increased knowledge suggest.

This analysis, focusing on change processes, seeks to be ideologically neutral. No alternative system, free or planned, is implied. On the contrary, it will be concluded that, because it is not possible to predict events or future system needs, it is not desirable to design lasting systems, institutions or policies. It is possible, however, to articulate behavioural principles to be observed if the goal is the prevention of conflict, violence and crime, and to discuss means of arriving at consensus goals of change and consensus processes of change.

The reality of interests

Any analysis such as this, along with the proposals that are the logical outcome of the analysis, remains idealism in the context of the existing power political 'realism'. Those who benefit from existing systems, and by definition these are those who are influential within systems, understandably resist change. Change processes are not possible unless this reality can be addressed.

There is, however, another reality. The 'realistic' power frame has within it the sources of self-destruction both of those who currently benefit from it and of civilizations. The 'idealistic' problem-solving and problem-provention frame becomes a practical option when the processes of change include means by which 'realists' can perceive and cost their present and future options accurately, resulting in some agreed shifts towards more secure national and international societies.

Presently the trends are very much in the other direction, with costly consequences. In developed economies the inabilities of governments to deal with emerging problems have led to strong trends towards handing over to the free market, almost regardless of the consequences. Failure by governments justifies this escape. At the international level, corporations are exploiting the underdeveloped world as ruthlessly as did colonialism. They are receiving the active support of national 'intelligence agencies' which, in the national interest, as defined by such agencies, seek to undermine other gov-

13

ernments which restrict penetration activities by these corporations.

It is now over a decade since Jonathan Kwitny, a reporter for the *Wall Street Journal*, exposed, as an example of the exercise of a colonial power, the activities of government agencies in the United States in his *Endless Enemies: The Making of an Unfriendly World*, with the sub-title 'How America's world-wide interventions destroy democracy and free enterprise and defeat our own best interests'.[4] The United States has engaged in wars that have been ruthlessly destructive of lives in Latin America, Asia and the Middle East. All seem to have been fought very much as a means of advancing US interests, including leaders' political interests, as seemed to be the case in Vietnam and later in Iraq where the military sought to overcome their sense of humiliation over Vietnam.

Education and consensus

The jump from we–they, adversarial, right–wrong traditions, still so dominant in legislatures, the law, industrial relations, and even family relations, to a mind-set that focuses more on human needs, reasoning and collaborative problem-solving, is a dramatic paradigm shift. With industrialization, it would seem, human intelligence has been used almost exclusively (with some minor exceptions such as in planning some token help to the poor and to poor nations) to promote short-term self-interest, rather than the longer-term interests of societies. Human intelligence remains an individual attribute unless structurally organized as a shared asset, as was more the case in early tribal societies. Ideally what is required in modern circumstances is a shift from a free-for-all short-term acquisition to some form of intellectually conditioned social evolution in which longer-term social cost calculations and reason dominate.

Some shifts in this direction are not necessarily idealism, for the felt needs are shared. The first would be to ensure that there are those who can conceptualize the jump and could include its nature in education generally. This implies an understanding of the language of Conflict Resolution and of its processes.[5] Required, also, are those who are trained to act as facilitators in helping management and decision-makers to identify problems and to assess accurately the future of institutional policies and processes. A new and important study and profession is called for.

The next shift would be to make this knowledge central in existing professions, particularly those involving education, law and economics, politics, sociology and others, so that a problem-solving orientation, rather than the power frame, becomes the foundation of professional activities. In a global society such as is now emerging, problem-solving approaches need to be observed by organizations such as the United Nations and its agencies, but this cannot happen until its member sovereign states have adjusted to the emerging global system and made their own cost assessments of their institutions and their power policies.

3) A further shift is for those who ultimately dominate political decision-making, including major international corporations, to play their part in joining the two seemingly opposing 'realities': the self-seeking realities, on the one hand, and the realities of consequential costs, on the other, especially the costs of depriving 20 per cent or so of a society of basic physical and social needs. Some fundamental shifts in policy are now required, and these will require shifts in institutions and processes to ensure that those directly concerned are represented in the decision-making process. There cannot be problem-solving processes unless all interests and needs are defined and catered for.

It is this utopian analytical frame which we examine in more depth in this Part, and within which in Part Two we examine in detail specific institutions, such as the family, leaderships, legislatures, public and civil services, legal systems, industrial organizations and others. This will lead in Part Three to an exploration of practical options and means of consensus change.

Notes

1   A. Rosenthal, *New York Times* (3 June 1994) quoting Professor John Dilulio of Princeton University.

2   R. Reich, *New York Times* (3 June 1994).

3   R. Coate and J. Rosati, *The Power of Human Needs* (Boulder CO, Lynne Reinner Publishers, 1988).

4   J. Kwitny, *Endless Enemies: The Making of an Unfriendly World* (New York, Congdon and Weed, 1984).

5   J. Burton, *Conflict Resolution: Its Language and Processes* (Lanham MD, Scarecrow Press, 1996).

3

Problems of compliance

A comprehensive approach to the failure of contemporary systems to deal with problems of conflict, violence and crime requires the bringing together of the three phenomena which are universal in civilizations. Problems of conflict are human problems. The first phenomenon is, therefore, the inherent nature of human beings and their ability, or lack of it, to conform to social norms and the institutions within which they live together. These norms and institutions have evolved over time as part of the ongoing struggle for survival and development, and include family conventions, leadership and community rivalries and competitive acquisitions. A second phenomenon is, therefore, the nature of social norms and institutions as they have now evolved. The third phenomenon is the compliance system that is administered by authorities to ensure observance of these norms and institutional requirements. Structures and compliance systems both vary greatly in different cultures and over time. In many societies military as well as police powers are employed to ensure compliance. The fact that compliance systems are required suggests that structures may frequently be incompatible with human capabilities and needs.

The assumption of aggressiveness

In discussing the human dimension there is a basic question we cannot afford to dodge. Are anti-social and violent behaviours due to inherent human aggressiveness derived from the consequences of primal evolution and the struggle for the survival of the fittest? Or is aggressiveness engendered by the adversarial institutions and norms which have evolved almost universally as a result of structures being imposed by elites on others, leading to adversarial we–they relations in primary, secondary and tertiary industries, and to class confrontations in politics and in society, which require compliance strategies?

A traditional and widespread view combines these two and holds that adversarial and interest-based management systems have evolved because by nature man is aggressive: the state and its institutions are aggressive because man is aggressive. The reality is that even if human aggressiveness is acquired, it is deeply ingrained because of the traditions of centuries past. It could date back to the origins of the separate family and its culture of control. Some would say that it makes little difference whether aggressiveness is inherent or acquired. In either case not much can be done about it.

Certainly, if inherent aggressiveness is the problem, then social problems just have to be lived with, while controlled as much as possible by police and deterrent strategies. But if, on the other hand, it is management conditions which stimulate this aggressiveness, then at least some reduction of conflict and violence would be possible if institutions could be adjusted to meet the needs of individuals and groups.

Theory and experience are now beginning to support this latter view. The man-is-aggressive or survival-of-the-fittest theory assumes that aggression is primarily in pursuit of material acquisition, especially resources and territories which are in limited supply. Experience and case studies, however, suggest that material acquisition is rarely the primary source of serious conflict. There is room for compromise in a dispute over physical acquisition, especially when there are likely to be costs of conflict. For this reason it has been possible to institutionalize legal, mediation and bargaining processes by which to handle disputes.

Our thinking, and indeed our language, has been confused by this traditional focus on material acquisition. As there has been little institutional interest in the emotions, values and non-material interests of the person, conflicts have been defined instead in physical terms. Matrimonial conflicts over custody and properties are defined in material terms though the real problem may be one of emotion. Workers strike over demands for increased wages even when the problem is one of relationships with management and treatment of the working person. International conflicts are defined as territorial even when there are clear independence or ethnic issues at stake. In all cases there are non-material needs to be satisfied that provoke such aggression, particularly the needs of personal status, recognition and identity. As will be recounted in a subsequent chapter, empirical evidence of this has led to a theory of needs and the development of conflict resolution as a basis for policy.

For reasons explored later, no bargaining or compromise, such as is possible with material acquisition, is possible in relation to any such deep-rooted human needs. Just as increased wages are not a permanent solution to many industrial disputes, so the dole is not acceptable compensation for the human costs of unemployment to young people seeking their identity in society, and anti-social behaviours may be a consequence. The right of a vote does not offset loss of ethnic identity by a minority within a majority-governed state. Secession demands persist. Threat and deterrent strategies are of no avail when human needs are being pursued.

So when Hans Morgenthau, in his power politics theory, attributed conflict to aggressiveness in physical acquisition, and deduced that conflicts can be avoided by threat and deterrent strategies, he omitted a human element that defeats his prescription.[1] He did not recognize any difference between 'disputes' (over physical resources) and 'conflicts' (over human needs and aspirations).

Such a view also misses out the basis for a positive approach. Unlike material needs, human needs of recognition and identity are not in short supply. Material resources must be shared, requiring bargaining and negotiation. But there is not necessarily any loss of a resource in giving a sense of identity to the person at the workplace, to young people, to minorities and to ethnic groups. There is no reason why human non-material needs should be a source of conflict once their existence is recognized and institutions are adjusted accordingly.

Our problem seems to be that non-material issues have not been regarded as important within the adversarial power institutions which societies have inherited. While there are institutional means of dealing with disputes over material issues – unsatisfactory because they are based on power bargaining – there are no formal procedures by which non-material issues can be dealt with. Legal cases involving domestic violence do not dig beneath the surface to reveal the consequences of traditional sex discriminations and some early childhood experiences. International mediation interventions carefully avoid consideration of ethnicity and identity problems created by arbitrary geographical boundaries inherited from colonialism and which would threaten existing state sovereignties if taken into account.

Within this frame it would seem that aggressiveness and conflicts within societies and between them are the direct result of some institutions and social norms being incompatible with inherent human needs. There is thus a circular process which over time increases aggressiveness and the need for increased compliance measures.

In the systems that have evolved over the last few thousand years, the struggle to survive and achieve has been very much a personal or class one, not a community one. These evolving competitive systems led to slavery, feudalism and forms of colonialism, and to present-day adversarial industrial and political relations. In our introductory chapter Lewis Mumford was quoted as writing 'the utopian ideal of total control from above, absolute obedience below, never entirely passed out of existence'. The difference now is that the power elite in developed societies is an extensive and politically influential middle class. This new power elite has not yet come to terms with the reality that as social and environmental conditions deteriorate further with the population doubling every thirty-five to forty years, individuals and conglomerates will act increasingly in their own interests. This will be at the further expense of others in their own and other societies. But ultimately, of course, it will be at their expense also as protest in the form of conflict and violence increases.

The neglect of a human dimension

Looking back on classical utopian thinking, and bearing in mind also the artificial constructs of the person such as 'economic man' and the 'socialized' member of society, and other such constructs of social science disciplines, it has to be observed that the study of human behaviour has been within a compliance frame. These constructs behave as required. This provides a basis for statistical prediction, but distorts analysis. Such constructs lead to the notion of 'dissidents', people behaving in an anti-social or abnormal way, which by implication threatens law and order in societies. Dissident behaviours are recorded statistically and there are constant media reports of particular cases. But until quite recently there has been little explanation of such behaviours besides references to aggressions, terrorism, violence and crime, as though these terms were explanatory. There has rarely been an analysis of the structural source of these behaviours or of the social conditions that might have led to them.

A moment's reflection makes this provocative observation self-evident and provides the reason. Within the traditional power politics frame in which social behaviours take place and are reported and analysed, human motivations and needs are not relevant. An authority, be it a dictator or the authority of democratic majority rule, has, if legitimized, a legal right to expect obedience. There is the traditional and consensus view that there are those who have a right to govern, and those who have an obligation to obey. The reserve powers are threat, coercion and punishment. These are means of control that have been regarded as appropriate and generally effective even in conditions in which there are obvious discriminations, deprivations and lack of developmental opportunities for some. It is assumed, first, that there can always be social conformity by personal choice and, second, that if necessary compliance can be enforced. Neither assumption is valid, as we shall see.

The reason why past compliance systems led to alienation and anti-social behaviours is now emerging. It is becoming clear that there are human limits to capacities to conform to elite-sponsored institutions and norms: the person is not wholly malleable. On the contrary, the needs that are frustrated by institutions *will* be pursued in one way or another. These needs would seem to be even more fundamental than food and shelter. Individuals are prepared to go to extreme lengths to defy systems in order to pursue their deeply felt needs, even death by suicide bombing or by hunger strikes. (We will later deal more explicitly with this vague notion of human needs.) Denial by society of personal recognition and identity leads, at all social levels, to alternative behaviours ranging from participation in street gangs, to dictatorial leadership,

Touch of this in domestic man/wife situation?

?

19

to terrorism. Many forms of protest have socially positive goals: under the pressure of this human protest colonialism has had to give place to more subtle forms of exploitation. Gender discrimination is being confronted. Industrial relations are undergoing change.

However, the assumption that people are to a large degree malleable and, therefore, can by choice conform with institutional practices and legal norms as required by authorities and society, remains unquestioned. If there is not such conformity, then the person is, again by choice, criminal or anti-social. This is an assumption hidden in the moral belief of 'social consciousness': there are those who are by nature and perhaps culture, immoral or anti-social, but they can be educated or coerced to behave as expected.

This assumption of an individual ability to conform has been applied at all societal levels and also at the international level. The possibility that the problems faced by modern civilizations could be due to their institutions imposing on citizens and nations norms of behaviour beyond human intellectual and emotional capacities, has not been widely considered.

There is, of course, a strong belief in justice and a just society. There always have been many who advocate political, economic and social change in the interests of justice. Violence, crime and anti-social behaviours, domestically, nationally and internationally, have been related to the existence of injustices. But the assumption that there can be conformity despite injustices, and that morally there should be such conformity pending change, has been general.

The limitations of scholarship

There are two reasons why scholars have not questioned this basic assumption of malleability. First, thinking occurs within an existing political consensus which few are inclined to challenge. There are intellectual arguments about legislative and legal processes, about whether punishment controls crime, about health, education, taxation and other such issues. But criminal and dissident behaviours are assessed in relation to existing institutions and norms. They are unquestionably treated as a deliberate defiance of them. Conventional philosophies, social theories and policies share the assumption that the person is wholly capable of accommodating the requirements of societies. Political psychology has a library of books such as *Socialization to Politics*[2] which deals with the role in socialization to be performed by the family, the school and the peer group, and *New Directions in Political Socialization*[3] which outlines steps which societies can take to ensure conformity. Why there must be this contrived socialization, why there is not conformity, is not usually explored.

Second, it has been assumed that the person is wholly malleable because the whole person has not been the subject of social studies. The separation of aspects of behaviours which occurred when knowledge was divided into disciplines at the end of the last century, established behavioural constructs which were designed to make possible accurate prediction, quantification and 'scientific' analysis, but which are far removed from reality.

Specializations have a narrow focus. By definition they must ignore complex human dimensions. Anyone who has had severe health problems knows how inadequate specializations can be, and how a specialist focus can lead to a false diagnosis. The law can punish within a given set of legal norms. But it is difficult to make judgements based on complex behavioural influences. Typically, punishment takes the place of treatment. Even treatment, if applied, is designed to ensure conformity with social norms, not with behavioural norms. What is required is a holistic approach that includes all aspects of behaviour and, also, all the features of the social circumstances in which behaviour takes place.

Within such a traditional consensus there has been a strong tendency for the majority of members of societies to accept the *status quo*, attributing its serious day-to-day problems to behavioural faults. The extent to which this is so has been documented by Philip Green. 'From cradle to grave we subsist in a world of unequal incentives and rewards, of sharply stratified and omnipresent hierarchy ... Not to fit into that structure is to claim, literally, the status of misfit.'[4] Traditional policies, including police and military controls, have been applied. High levels of long-term unemployment, poverty, widespread alienation and its consequences have remained without any attempt to assess the social costs of these conditions and to invest in change.

Institutions and human aspirations

Institutions are the result of history – the evolution of societies. Societies evolved within a power frame. In due course there were consolidations brought about by constitutions and processes designed to ensure law and order. There were also expansions brought about by explorations, migrations, colonialism and aggressions, with their own behavioural consequences. Institutions to this day reflect this past, and especially the ways in which more powerful interests dominate. Behaviour, on the other hand, is the result, not of institutional history, but of the gradual evolution of inherent human drives and abilities designed to equip the individual for appropriate roles in human relationships and in the physical environment.

But societies are no longer face-to-face communities in which personal roles are assured. The competitive stage of human history has led to conditions in which a social role, and the personal identity that goes with it, are no longer assured. It does not follow, therefore, that the system that has resulted any longer directs such inherent drives towards conforming social behaviours. The same drives that led to social roles can readily lead to violent leadership contests and to property acquisition rather than to social cohesion. As a consequence, the majority of people have had no adequate outlets for their social pursuits. They have been merely observers or victims in the power struggles that have taken place over the ages.

There are, therefore, two very different forces to be analysed. As has been observed, on the one hand, there are individual and group aspirations being pursued, reflecting inherent human needs for recognition and identity. On the other, there are social norms and institutions that have evolved, nationally and internationally, as a result of the pursuit by the more influential members of societies of their political, economic and social interests. Those previously powerless people who have been denied their aspirations and needs frequently now have available to them effective means of protest.

The historical context

More recent political and social change has failed to bring these two forces together, perhaps largely because there has been no perceived immediate political need for this to happen within the traditional power frame.

Historically this is not difficult to understand. Contemporary societies are not far removed in time from extreme authoritative systems. The industrial revolution transferred feudalism in its various we–they forms from the land to industry. Legislative systems reflected this. In England the emerging 'democracy' retained a House of Lords, while the merchant class remained strongly represented in the dominant House of Commons, and until recent times 'suffrage' was only for males with a certain property qualification. Compulsory voting exists in only a few countries, such as in Australia. In the most democratic and economically developed of countries the we–they, interest-oriented power relationships remain in legislatures, courts, the workplace and the home, with only slight modifications over the years.

The human race depicts itself as being above other species in that it has a measure of intelligent self-determination and self-development. Certainly the human capacity for technological invention has led to a continuing transformation of living conditions. Nevertheless, little has changed in the nature of social relationships. Even many of those whose role it is to deal with problems of personal adjustment to societies, such as social workers and psychologists, have, like those in the fields of politics, economics and law, largely ignored the human factor, giving priority to helping their clients to conform to institutions and social norms. The person who is 'normal' is one who conforms to the social norms of the system and who accepts a way of life determined by the economic and financial norms of the system. Others are categorized as abnormal or neurotic. Far from directing social evolution in the interests of all members of societies, and thereby promoting a mutually beneficial future, intellectual capacities have been devoted far more to preserving the inherited institutions and norms. In particular, the family has been regarded as private and sacrosanct, not subject to social control.

This is not to deny a continuing concern about the plight of unrepresented and deprived people in societies. There has been a continuing intellectual interest in *Human Nature in Politics*[5] and in *Psychological Needs and Political Behavior.*[6] There has been an interest in the quite fundamental problems of majority government that lead to the alienation of minorities, as, for example, *Beyond Adversary Democracy.*[7] But these interests and concerns are a recognition of injustices within existing societies that ideally should be removed. They do not acknowledge behavioural realities and the costly and self-defeating nature of existing institutions which do not accommodate human requirements. The result is that these studies argue what ought to happen as a matter of justice, not what will inevitably happen as a consequence of the denial of human needs, itself an extreme injustice.

Malleability by punishment

Arising out of this disregard for human behaviour and the assumption that it is sufficiently malleable, is the further assumption that when threats are not heeded, punishments will lead to future conformity. This is the approach to domestic crime, where imprisonment is a punishment. It is also the approach to international power politics where sanctions and military invasions are still thought to be the means of control. Both are applied in the absence of insights into the reasons for defiance of social or international norms. When compliance is strategy the values, motivations, needs and aspirations that inspire the 'culprits' are not treated as relevant.

An extensive theoretical and empirical literature has provided strong evidence that punishment does not stop further crime and, on the contrary, accentuates it. But the lack of institutionalized alternatives, together with a social desire for revenge, has led to such evidence being ignored.

This focus on the individual as the cause of social problems has led, in addition to coercive remedies, to court-ordered therapy and even to sympathy and tolerance of the individual in many cases that come before courts. There are support groups to help dissidents. But rarely do courts, or well-meaning social organizations, direct attention to the institutional frame in which the dissidence took place and the actual sources of that dissidence. No amount of sympathy, idealism or support for the individuals, who happen to be caught breaking the legal norms of the system, can solve ongoing social problems that have an institutional base. For every individual treated there will be many others breaking the law or social norms. Nor can such sympathy or support reduce the costs of violence.

In short, vested interests in existing systems as they have evolved, and wider security interests in the preservation of the *status quo*, have perpetuated a reluctance to believe that citizens may not be malleable and capable of adjustment to existing social norms. The idea is not entertained that people as individuals and as members of communities do not necessarily behave as is expected of good citizens in divided societies, not because of a lack of social consciousness, but through an inherent inability to accept alienation, which results from a genetic need for social integration. To entertain such a thought would imply that institutions might have to adapt to the needs of people, not for reasons of justice or democracy, but for the reason that people cannot adjust to those institutions which establish conditions which are incompatible with human needs. All of this is a bit nebulous – until one explores *with* terrorists, military dictators and others who confront social norms just what motivates them.

A wider perspective

Some decades ago, following the Second World War, there were independence movements world-wide. The British, the Dutch, the French and other colonial nations were powerless to contain post-war demands for separate autonomies throughout Asia and Africa. Later, the United States and its allies were defeated in North Korea and then in Vietnam, which was struggling for a real independence in the place of the post-colonial government put into place by the outgoing French.

Were not these demands for recognition and autonomy the same as are now being made at all social levels, in all societies? Women have been struggling for equality in society and the workplace for many generations and the struggle continues. In industrial relations employees still demand to be treated as people. Ethnic groups seek independence and autonomy. Teenagers experience frustration in finding a role in society, especially when denied adequate educational and occupational opportunities. The symptoms are perhaps most evident in the behaviours of frustrated youth. As one reporter has stated, 'The grunge fashion is a way they say "this is how I feel about what you've done to my life" – they are expressing anger towards their lack of opportunities.'[8] Just as local authorities treat violence as behaviour to be repressed with little examination of its roots, so ethnic conflicts within and between nation-states, war-lord violence and repressive military regimes are still viewed by the United Nations as phenomena to be repressed rather than explained. They are treated accordingly. 'Peace-making' and 'peace-keeping', which seek to maintain the *status quo*, are still the attempted, though unsuccessful, means of control. There is, clearly, some social force arising out of human behaviours that challenges authorities at all social levels, domestic and international, and in all cultures. It defies social and legal norms and existing institutions. Defining that force must be a precondition of prevention.

Society and the individual

It should not be concluded from the above that this emphasis on the individual implies that the interests of a community or society are to be sacrificed. On the contrary, societies are collaborative and harmonious to the extent that they are made up of persons who have a common sense of purpose and of security. The emphasis is on the human needs of the person, but the goal is the integration of the society.

This has a special application in relation to ethnic minorities. There is a strong tendency amongst liberal-minded people to favour integration over separate autonomies. Separation is associated with uncooperative and extreme minorities. But the same reasoning applies to communities as to individuals. If the minorities are placed in a setting in which they have an identity and feel secure, such as a separate autonomy, they can reach out and establish positive functional relationships with other communities. If placed in a situation of uncertainty and fear due to a lack of effective representation, there can be little social integration.

Recognizing and being supportive of the realities of ethnicity and the struggles to preserve it rather than to promote a 'multicultural' society is not 'racist' as many would argue. Ethnicity is an important means of seeking the recognition and identity of the individual in circumstances in which they are denied. Separate autonomies are to be encouraged in many situations in the post-colonial world in which artificial boundaries are still being preserved. The desirable alternative is a society so structured that all its members have developmental and role opportunities which provide for personal identity. This, however, is rarely possible, at least in the short term. Societies continue to have class and alienation problems.

In many cases ethnic conflict, leading to demands for autonomy, are sponsored by leadership ambitions and rivalries. Africa is going through a stage of intense conflict in which the post-colonial boundaries give opportunities for leadership rivalries based on tribalism. Peoples are caught up in the struggles and have no option but to join in the tribalism, despite many inter-marriages and harmonious community relationships. In short, the historical pursuit of power by individuals seeking leadership status, megalomania and unbridled ambition may be a direct outcome of structural conditions. Such behaviours, resulting from denied identity and an adequate social role, lead to a dictatorial denial to the majority of citizens of their personal recognition and status – a vicious circle.

From power theories to behavioural realities

Power theories are valid in explaining the growth of societies and their institutions. But they have also been used as a basis of policy, arguing that through power there can be law and order and international stability. Because institutions emerged within a power frame, it has incorrectly been assumed that power controls individual behaviours, that deterrence reliably deters even when non-negotiable human needs are being pursued. This is a false and unjustified extension of power theories. Failed deterrence threats have been followed by wars. Police and armed forces have not been able to control ethnic violence. But the attempts are an application of the power theories which still dominate social science disciplines.

If we are to deal with problems of societies we cannot afford to work within a construct that assumes certain institutional givens, but disregards human aspirations and ontological needs. It is true that human aspirations can be and have been repressed over periods of time. But emerging conditions, especially population increases, rapid and universal communications and the widespread availability of means of violence, are making it increasingly difficult for authorities to impose traditional institutional norms that frustrate human aspirations.

Recognition of the uncontrollable power of some dissident behaviours is not an intellectual surrender to widespread violence in confronting authorities. It is an acknowledgement that these unacceptable and uncontrollable realities must be explained, not brushed aside or suppressed. Only then can appropriate remedies be discovered.

Accepting realities, recognizing the power of human behaviours as expressed in universal violence at all social levels, is a major challenge to social science disciplines, to traditional legal norms and to most institutions in political and social life, including those that govern behaviour in the family and the workplace. In recent years there have been some changes in thinking as individuals have joined together to assert the identity of the person. But the belief that, with sufficient coercion, the person is malleable, has not been seriously challenged. 'Man is aggressive', 'man is xenophobic' and other such theses, which are convenient in that they justify authoritative controls, seem, in the light of experience, to be dangerously superficial. We are finally being forced to reconsider the sources of historical violence and conflicts.

Different possibilities have to be examined. Perhaps the person, otherwise co-operative and valuing social relationships, has been forced, by an institutional framework, to be aggressive in self-defence. Perhaps institutions, developed as a result of past leadership interests, while satisfying the human aspirations of some, deny them to too many others. It may be that there are human relationship needs, no less vital than food and shelter, that will be fought for accordingly. Perhaps, if co-operative and non-violent social relationships are sought by societies, social norms and institutions must be adapted to human aspirations and not the other way around.

Cultural variables

The idea that there are human needs for identity which are frustrated by societies as they have evolved worries some anthropologists. Certainly in some face-to-face communities the pursuit of identity was not a problem: the individual identified with the tribe, and later in early agricultural days, with the extended family or social class.

Group child-care, hunting, ceremonial tribal conflicts and traditional communal activities provided opportunities for activities which provided the person with a role. But with the emergence of industries and cities, social structures no longer provided opportunities for all members of societies to play a role. Present trends in democratic and developed societies, including high levels of youth unemployment, a failure to provide minorities with opportunities for participation in political decision-making processes, reduced resources available for education and health, and other related conditions, seem to be establishing structures likely to lead to increased frustrations in the pursuit of personal identity.

Terrorism

Those who have worked in conflict situations with 'terrorists' and leaders of organizations involved in violence and crime are aware of the influence of structural conditions and the way in which a peaceful protest situation tends to move in the direction of threat and violence when no progress is made. In Northern Ireland violence had its origins in peaceful protest which in due course escalated into widespread violence and terrorism. From time to time there were periods of quiet while negotiations were anticipated, only to revert back to violence when no progress was made. The leaders of the opposing Protestant and Catholic factions have been ordinary citizens, caring for their families and living their lives as wholly normal persons. Many of their more active followers were also ordinary citizens who in due course had a vested interest in the continuation of the conflict in that without it they would have no social role or identity, and no job or income. The perception we have of 'terrorists' is that of persons who are abnormal and disturbed and who need to be removed from society. Yet in fact they have, typically, more than average intelligence, but frequently have been deprived of educational and career opportunities. The role their activities provide gives them an identity, and the more active they are, the more risks they take, the greater respect they acquire. As Richard Rubenstein observed: 'One need have very little sympathy for terrorists to insist that they are neither brutes nor devils, but people in many ways like us.' In his conclusions he observes, 'it seems to me that our policy must be to uproot the causes of terrorism by putting an end to ... oppression of classes, nations, and ethnic communities'.[9]

This same analysis applies to many leadership roles, especially those provided by a military coup. In due course leaders fear the possibilities of rival take-overs and become paranoiac and ruthless in eliminating possible threats. If these same people had early opportunities of development in other professions and careers, giving social recognition, they would probably have been ordinary citizens, condemning just those behaviours they now follow. Even at the party political level there are the same behavioural features. If politics were not adversarial, a different type of person would be attracted and a different behavioural pattern would emerge.

Identity is sought in different cultures and circumstances in different ways. Except in conditions of extreme deprivation of physical needs promoting apathy and acceptance, the pursuit of identity cannot be contained. The person who has had the opportunity to develop fully and to play a respected social role can readily adjust to relationships in a foreign ethnic, religious or political environment. The frustrated person, on the other hand, will seek identity through a familiar identity group, or if necessary invent one, such as a new religious order with some special belief system.

This reference to extreme cases has been made merely to stress the need in societies for opportunities, especially for children and young people, to develop fully their potential and to find suitable roles in society.

Domestic violence

In this analysis different social levels have been treated as one, on the grounds that at all levels there is a common human response to structural and social circumstances which frustrate human needs. The analysis seeks to explain conflict, whether it be at the family, the national or the international level. The connection will sometimes be hard to see, especially for those who have had direct experiences at some particular level. Is family violence behaviourally the same, does it have the same source, as dictatorial leadership violence? Could not a violent dictator be a co-operative and considerate partner, or a democratic representative be a domestic tyrant? We are examining behaviour within the frame of a human need for identity and recognition, and security of that identity and recognition. We know that a dictator will go to almost any lengths to ensure the security of his or her role. This need not be a sign of an aggressive personality. The same person in another social setting could present a very different image, for example in an international setting in which accommodations must sometimes be made to more powerful others. We return to this subject in Part Two when discussing the family as a social institution.

The importance of taking this wider perspective is to avoid defining particular cases by reference only to apparent personality problems before determining their sources. Parents have difficulty in determining the reasons for apparently aggressive behaviours by their children, but, nevertheless, apply restraints, which are likely to accentuate such behaviours. Societies apply punishments for proven violence and crimes without determining the reasons for these behaviours. The problems remain.

Abnormalities

There is, of course, the problem of abnormalities. This is a difficult area to discuss as there is little consensus. Psychoanalysts have recognized how social conditions frustrate human needs. The needs to which they refer are treated within the need for development. Psychological and psychiatric analysts have, as a result of clinical experience, been led to conclude that the personal struggle for recognition and identity is an inherent one. Because their clients are individuals, they focus on an analysis of the person. But while they are fully aware of the way in which the social environment prevents human development and destroys the integrity of persons, they apparently feel no competence or opportunity to make an analysis of that environment and to suggest appropriate changes in it. Rather, the obligation remains on the person to adjust. Non-conformity can be defined by reference to social norms and attributed to some inherent personal attributes, but non-conformity it is. It is the task of the psychoanalyst to help the individual to conform. The analysis is, however, limited to the person, sometimes necessarily extending to the family, but rarely to society and to social systems as a whole.

This is not to deny, of course, the reality of some individual abnormalities that might be chemical or physical in origin, some of which lead to dangerously aggressive behaviours. There are, also, those deep-rooted abnormalities that probably are a by-product of early family and environmental experiences and which result in continuing anti-social behaviours. There is probably some continuity in these physically and socially determined behaviours, but there is little doubt that social conditions are a major factor even in forms of behaviour that might be classified as chemical or physical. For example, there are cases of terrorism which relate directly to activities associated with the Vietnam war, carried out by persons who otherwise lead admirable lives. There are many cases of family violence that appear to be due to severe abnormalities, but which involve persons with wartime experiences which have been suppressed.[10] There is no option but the physical containment of those who commit violent crimes, accompanied by some forms of treatment.

But the existence of 'abnormal' behaviours should not divert attention from types of anti-social behaviours that are widespread and which seem to be related to unacceptable conditions, such as robberies, frequently and inevitably violent. There may be an overlap between the genetically abnormal and anti-social behaviours that stem from social conditions. It is, neverthe-

29

less, reasonable to separate individual abnormalities from behaviours of persons who might be responding by anti-social behaviours and even terrorism to unacceptable circumstances.

There are also individuals who must be regarded as normal and with no apparent excuse for committing some crime, as, for example, international drug-peddling or robbing a corporation of large amounts of money. Such crimes fit well into a private enterprise system and are probably also widespread in other systems. Systems must have rules, and rules must be observed. Punishments are sometimes appropriate. The focus in this study is, however, not on abnormal behaviours and not on rule-breaking by persons who seek to exploit opportunities for material gain within a system. The focus is on those behaviours that occur as a result of a conflict between institutions and human needs. The probability is that they can be treated only by adjusting systems to the needs of their members.

The search for cause or explanation

In July 1992 the *New York Times* published a series of well-researched articles on poverty. It surveyed relief systems designed to help the poor. These articles were unusual in their recognition of the social realities of poverty and alienation, and public attitudes to welfare assistance. They stressed the need for far more assistance to the alarming proportion of the population that was below the poverty line. But the underlying assumption of the articles was the underlying assumption of the welfare policies under review: the problem of poverty had to be treated by welfare. There was little recognition of the need to deal with the sources of problems of poverty: systems and policies that lead to unemployment, lack of training opportunities and inadequate health-care.

This is not to deny that many of societies' problems can be and are dealt with effectively by direct interventions. Scurvy was once a disease associated with sailors, with implications of lack of cleanliness. So much was this the case that the word scurvy came to imply dishonourable or contemptible. It was a persistent and expensive disease. Accidental discovery of a simple remedy, lime juice, provided a means of prevention. So it is, also, with many specific problems that plague societies. Like mechanical problems they can be treated outside any ideological or value-oriented frame. But societies are plagued by problems for which there is as yet no agreed cause – social and ethnic violence, child abuse, wars between war-lords, and others – and, therefore, no agreed remedies.

In practice, once a simple cause is discovered there are usually few intellectual problems in reaching agreement on remedies. In retrospect, the problem is not as complex as was previously thought. In other words, failure to discover and to agree on cause prevents agreement on remedies and leads to ideological conflict even between those who might genuinely seek remedies.

Failure to discover and agree on causes leads to a frustrated acceptance of that which exists. It leads to the policy of containment of problems, often by official violence.

Causes of social problems such as conflict and violence are, however, of such a fundamental nature that they are the common source of many seemingly different problems. There are few social problems for which a simple and separate lime juice remedy would be the answer.

A book such as this on the subject of failed political, economic and social systems and failed relationships generally, makes no contribution to thinking unless it contributes significantly to the discovery of causes. It is for this reason that this Part has sought to provide this behavioural frame of analysis, hypothesizing that structural violence is the source of conflict and violence whenever conditions deny to people and to their identity groups a role in society which gives personal recognition and a sense of belonging. Within this behavioural frame we can now, in Part Two, examine the institutions of society to see to what extent they deny to citizens the satisfaction of their human needs.

From a holistic perspective, however, the frame provides a simple lime juice answer in the sense that problems of violence can be traced to the pursuit of human needs of recognition and identity, and the sense of security they provide. These are social commodities which increase with personal acquisition and in theory there should be no social problem in satisfying them. Earlier social systems managed it. Not so simplistic will be an analysis of the changes which would seem to be required in existing institutions (Part Two), and the means by which necessary change can be brought about (Part Three). But first we must delve a little more into the concept of human needs.

Notes

1   H. Morgenthau, *Politics Among Nations: The Struggle for Power and Peace* (New York, Knopf, 1948).
2   D. Jaros, *Socialization to Politics* (Westport CT, Praeger, 1973).
3   D. and S. Schwartz, eds, *New Directions in Political Socialization* (New York, Free Press, 1975).
4   P. Green, *The Pursuit of Inequality* (New York, Pantheon, 1981).
5   J. Davies, *Human Nature in Politics: The Dynamics of Political Behavior* (New York, John Wiley, 1963).
6   S. Renshon, *Psychological Needs and Political Behavior: A Theory of Personality and Political Efficacy* (New York, Free Press, 1974).
7   J. Mansbridge, *Beyond Adversary Democracy* (New York, Basic Books, 1980).
8   E. Blake, *Sydney Morning Herald* (21 December 1993).
9   R. Rubenstein, *Alchemists of Revolution: Terrorism in the Modern World* (New York, Basic Books, 1987).
10 J. S. Dryzek, *Discursive Democracy* (Cambridge, Cambridge University Press, 1990).

4

Needs theory

This is quite a decent summary of what has been said

The last chapter was based on the provocative assumption that there are certain ontological human needs that *will* be pursued, that they provide a power greater than police and military power, that they lead the individual and identity group to defy compliance requirements, and that they explain and even justify in some circumstances anti-social and violent behaviours.

The assumption of human needs is so crucial to the analysis which will follow that it must be given more substance and justification.

Deprivations and 'structural violence'

Circumstances sometimes impose deprivations on people and communities about which little can be done by those affected. Sometimes such deprivations are due to conditions over which there can be no control, such as accidents and unavoidable weather and environmental conditions. It is in such circumstances that others contribute assistance.

'Structural violence', by contrast, is a term used to describe damaging deprivations caused by the nature of social institutions and policies. As such it is, by definition, an avoidable, perhaps a deliberate violence against the person or community. Structural violence is sometimes associated with some specific acts, such as economic sanctions and discriminations imposed on people. More generally, structural violence results from compliance processes, perceived injustices, and deprivations such as an absence of job opportunities. There are also much more damaging instances, such as starvation and deprivations experienced in civil wars. The origins of structural violence are, therefore, the policy and administrative decisions that are made by some and which adversely affect others.

Societies and institutions within them have degrees of structural violence which are endemic. In a complex social organization, be it a society or a large factory, there is frequently limited face-to-face contact. For organizational reasons there must be those who have leadership roles and those over whom they exercise authority. The former do not know the latter as personalities:

they are units within a system. The latter, like the machines they operate, are required to observe behavioural norms and practices determined by those in authority. Unless the organization is democratic in the widest participatory sense, these norms inevitably tend to accommodate institutional or organizational interests, with insufficient knowledge or consideration of those affected, giving rise to structural violence.

All industrial societies, as they have evolved, have this feature, stemming from the physical separation of those who are in authority and those who are required to conform. The system being administered, whether it be the political and social system as a whole or a particular enterprise, is administered in the belief that it is the appropriate one, and conformity is expected. Furthermore, whether the system has known defects or not, the belief is that required behaviours can be enforced if necessary.

At a political level apathy and withdrawal are interpreted as a willingness to accept systems, even though alienation – an emotional response to structural violence – is experienced. When 50 per cent or so of citizens do not take part in an electoral process, as in the United States where voting is not compulsory, it is likely that this is not acceptance, but a sense of alienation. Such alienation is frequently accompanied by protest forms of behaviour, such as the formation of alternative groups with which to identify.

A false interpretation of apathy leads those who achieve leadership and elite status to assume that, subject to some negotiation, they can exercise control. The belief that law and order in a society can be enforced is a belief that is deeply ingrained in the thinking of societies that have evolved within a power frame. That compliance can be enforced, that deterrence deters, is a proposition that has had wide acceptance.

The human-needs frame of analysis is based on the proposition that, while structural violence is a reality, while, that is, there is a large degree of forced compliance, there are situations and conditions which are beyond the capability of the person or identity group to accommodate. There are human needs that *will* be pursued. In response to structural violence there will be resistance to the imposed conditions, violent resistance if necessary.

The concept of structural deprivation and violence is relevant to institutions throughout systems, including not only the workplace, but importantly the family. The family is a social institution in which in most cultures the male spouse has had, traditionally, a dominant role, and in which parents, usually untutored in parenting, frequently impose compliance measures upon their children which are destructive of development and a sense of identity. Domestic violence, the sexual abuse of children and physical abuse even within the frame of learning and obedience, are all examples of structural violence. In Part Two it will be argued that responses include, in the longer term, many forms of anti-social behaviours in society, in the workplace and in political activities, even in important leadership roles.

Structures and human needs

If there are fundamental drives that the individual and identity group cannot voluntarily contain, then it cannot be assumed that law and order can be enforced except in conditions in which protest behaviours are physically impossible – as in slavery. The whole basis of law and order and organizational control are threatened in any circumstances in which such drives are frustrated.

This is, therefore, the fundamental question to pose: are there some human needs that *will* be pursued, regardless of consequences, that destroy the major premise of civilizations – that deterrence deters? If the answer is yes, then there must be a challenging paradigm shift in thinking and in decision-making at all system levels.

Experience suggests that this is the case: there are clear limits to abilities willingly to conform. The young person leaving school can expect and accept problems in finding employment for the first time. But continuing unemployment, leading to a sense of being a nobody and to experiencing alienation, is unacceptable. Under such circumstances adjustment within the norms of society is not possible in the absence of extensive family and social support. Suicide, theft, street gangs, violence against migrants and competitive ethnic groups, are understandable responses. The member of an ethnic minority who experiences discrimination, in addition to other threats to identity and recognition as a person, may be even more likely to act recklessly, to follow terrorist leaderships and to seek achievement in anti-social and subversive ways. Most damaging of all is the transfer of anger by those who feel deprived, not against those responsible, for they are not accessible, but against others within a community also suffering, such as other minorities, and even others who live in the same locality.

Remote we–they authority relationships are a common feature of modern societies as they have evolved. We–they relationships dominate legislatures, legal systems and the workplace. The norms of such relationships inevitably extend even to face-to-face relationships, as in the home, where frequently a parent, having been brought up in a tense relationship or having lost opportunities for identity at the workplace, seeks to gain it by dominating behaviours. Dominating behaviours come to be admired. Political leaders score points with their electorates if they are seen to be tough on foreign nations when they do not conform with demands made to them. Examples of collaborative activities, such as small community organizations with agreed goals as in volunteer fire-fighting, or employee ownership of enterprises, exist and are popular, but they are by no means dominant.

The evolution of needs theory

In structural violence there is no identifiable culprit, but there are victims. In the 1960s Johan Galtung posed the question, who are the 'criminals' behind this violence? He wrote extensively seeking to identify those who cause structural violence.[1]

Soon after Galtung's contribution, conflict resolution processes were developed, initially at the international level. *Needs theory* became a short-hand way of describing the problems created by structural violence and pointed more directly to ways in which they could be tackled. The onus of responsibility for dealing with problems of structural violence was on those who had the greatest influence within the system. They, too, would suffer in the longer term if the problems were not resolved. Thirty years later the exponential increase in conflict, violence and crime universally, at levels from the family to the inter-ethnic and the international, is leaving the real 'criminals' with no constructive option but, in their own interests, to become involved in problem-solving through conflict resolution processes in which all parties affected must play a part.

What needs theory did was to direct attention to a distinction between *negotiable interests* and *non-negotiable needs*, between disputes and conflicts. The former could be dealt with by legal and bargaining processes. Non-negotiable needs, on the other hand, required processes that would lead to altered perceptions by the parties concerned, and in some cases agreed structural change.

Clarity is required on the term 'human needs'. It should not be confused with 'human rights'. The US Government in the 1990s tried to force China to observe certain human rights, such as the right to protest, threatening to limit trading opportunities if this were not done. 'Rights' in the United States do not include the right of a job, or the right to have a living, or the practical, as distinct from the legal, right not to suffer discriminations. In democracies claims are made for the right of assembly, of expression, of choice. There could be societies which did not include these opportunities for political and social participation, but which, nevertheless, were acceptable to their members in given developmental circumstances. Even in democracies such rights are curbed in times of an emergency, such as war. 'Rights' have a cultural connotation, usually associated with particular systems of government.

The distinctive feature of 'needs', on the other hand, is that they are assumed to be inherent in human beings and in other species also and, therefore, universal and not just cultural. It is for this reason that those working within *needs theory* (see below) consider it appropriate to generalize across cultures and across societal levels from the interpersonal and family to the international.

Such needs have long been recognized. Abraham Maslow, in his *Towards a*

Psychology of Being, had a list of needs ranging from the physical, such as food and shelter, to relationship needs.[2] He implied that it was the physical needs that were sought first. But more recent studies suggest that relationship needs are sometimes sought at the sacrifice of physical needs and even of life itself.

There are other writers, such as Renshon, whose concern is far more with psychological needs being met in political systems.[3] Renshon stresses the need for personal control, a useful broad concept, and makes an analysis of political behaviours. He comes up with a series of realistic propositions that deal with behaviour at all social levels from the family to the political. They are based on replies to questionnaires sent to relevant groups. The impact of experience at all social levels is examined, leading to important insights into political attitudes and behaviours. Davies makes an extensive review of needs theorists, especially those whose views have a relevance to political participation and apathy.[4]

The power of human needs

An early recognition of the power of human needs was expressed in 1973, when Paul Sites wrote a book entitled *Control: The Basis of Social Order*.[5] The control to which he was referring was not control by authorities, but the control that persons exercise by reason of their inherent drives. Subsequently he referred to 'Needs as Analogues of Emotions'.[6]

At an international conference, held in Berlin in 1979, consideration was given to human needs by a group of scholars drawn from various disciplines, seeking a better understanding of human relationships. Their papers, *Human Needs*, edited by Katrin Lederer, were published in 1980.[7] Many of these same scholars met in 1989 with others interested in the nature of conflict and its resolution. Within this conflict frame there was no idealism attached to the desirability of observing human needs. It was a straightforward costing orientation: if needs were not satisfied there would be costly conflicts. Inherent needs for recognition, identity and security (more a psychological security than a physical one) were emphasized in their papers.

It was interesting that the initial Human Needs scholars, while searching for a theoretical frame for their sociological interests, did not directly relate their thinking to the issue of conflict. Nor had those in the Conflict Resolution field previously considered the Human Needs frame as that which would enable them to develop their thinking from immediate conflict resolution thinking to future problem prevention by appropriate policies which took account of needs. The experience made possible a 'Conflict Series' of four books, published in 1990, one of which included the papers of the 1989 conference referred to above.[8]

These experiences suggest that terms such as identity and recognition require far more definition than concepts and language presently make possi-

So human need was recognised and then people exercise because of their inherent drives, but at that point it was not linked to conflict. Burton's work previously built on the earlier work

ble. Nevertheless, the conceptual frame is there. The implications are far-reaching. If a need for recognition and identity is inherent, or deeply in-grained in human nature, then obviously there will be every endeavour, by whatever means are available, to achieve it. The inherent human needs concept explains why persons identify with ethnic groups that seek their separate autonomies and why they denigrate peoples of other cultures. By reference to them, one can explain the source of street gangs and their claims for territory. Light is thrown on some aggressive leadership behaviours. One can understand why threat and coercion will not in all circumstances curb behaviours, even in the short term, and why they could further stimulate violent responses.

Malleable or compelling?

This literature, however, does not deal with the question posed above, whether needs can be controlled in ways that allow for social conformity, or whether coercion and deterrence must fail in some circumstances. For the purposes of this analysis, just how needs are defined is not a major issue. Some summary notion such as personal control, or recognition and identity, is probably adequate for our purposes. The issue of concern is whether such needs can be suppressed and whether, therefore, citizens can become subject to control by authorities, or whether needs remain a power unto themselves, not subject to control by the individual, placing the individual outside the control of authorities. It is this nature of needs that is of concern rather than a precise definition and listing of them.

By inherent or basic, terms used interchangeably in many writings, is meant deep-rooted – nothing will change such a need. It will be pursued regardless of cost. Whether this is due to a natural instinct, or to a very early acquisition in some species, is a difficult biological question to answer. It is not an issue that need concern us. Our concern is whether there are some aspirations or needs that *will* be pursued, regardless of consequences, at least when basic physical needs have been met so that total apathy does not exist.

The empirical evidence seems to be clear: there are so many examples of needs of identity leading to tremendous outpourings of time and energy in the pursuit of some social or interest goal, and so many examples of frustrated needs leading to alienation or revenge-type behaviours. Religious and ethnic conflicts are examples of the pursuit of such needs. Perhaps the most convincing empirical evidence comes, however, from doctors who deal with cases of violence and have the opportunity to explore, not only the nature of human needs, but why it is that they are compelling. In *Deadly Consequences: How Violence is Destroying Our Teenage Population and a Plan to Begin Solving the Problem*,[9] Dr Deborah Prothrow-Smith reviews her research into the chemical responses to frustration and violence. This is a complex subject and further research is called for; but it does seem that the deductive hypothesis of the Needs Theorists has support in studies of the chemistry of the brain.

Needs theory and organizational problems

An issue of concern in an analysis of social problems at all system levels, from the family to the international, is not just the existence of these human needs. It is important to determine whether people in their adult lives, and in their social and political responses in the family, in the workplace, and in leadership roles nationally and internationally, are responding to the same needs. Is it possible to generalize across social levels, from person to person, nation to nation, assuming the same needs, even though the circumstances and responses seem so different? Should separate disciplines, dealing with social interactions at different social levels, assume the same human needs? If human needs were satisfied, would serious violence at all social levels then be avoided?

As has been observed, disciplines have been separated out from the total body of knowledge by reference to social levels: the person (Psychology), societies (Sociology), political groupings (Politics) and global relationships (International Relations). Those identifying with these separate fields tend to have their own special frames. They claim that separate studies are justified because behaviour at different social levels is different. But this may be a mistake. The need for identity may find expression in person-to-person relationships in ways different from those in group relationships, but while forms will differ, the drives for identity are experienced regardless of social level.

The conclusion to which we are coming is that seemingly different and separate social problems, from street violence to industrial frictions, to ethnic and international conflicts, are symptoms of the same cause: institutional denial of needs of recognition and identity, and the sense of security provided when they are satisfied, despite losses though violent conflict.

This conclusion may not relate to the personal experience of many of those who take an intellectual interest in these problems. Professionally they have their identity and their security. They can cross cultural and ethnic boundary lines without feeling threatened. They are not subject to discriminations. This probably explains why such people take a 'liberal' view on the integration of ethnic minorities by one-person-one-vote processes, as was the case in South Africa in 1994. If they suffered acutely from the frustration of human needs that touches the identity and security of the person, then they might adopt a different analytical approach. It would be one that sought to get to the roots of the problem. In an ethnic conflict situation the 'liberal' view would then be to provide some form of separate autonomies, especially in cases in which communities were in separate regions. Such communities would then feel more secure and would make close functional relationships with others.

Needs and problem-solving

This chapter has been concerned with the behavioural component – human needs – of the analysis of conflict, violence and crime. The behavioural component has been introduced, not for any value or idealistic reason, but for practical cost reasons. It may be that the theoretical frame is still incomplete; but what seems clear is that compliance strategies and deterrence measures can no longer be claimed as an effective means by which to control behaviours. They are, therefore, costly in their consequences. Recognizing the costs of not accommodating this behavioural component provides a motivation for change.

The alternative to authoritative compliance and to structural violence is, in the specific case, the bringing together in an analytical frame the offenders and those who represent the economic-political-social structures and norms with which offenders seem to be in conflict. This analytical problem-solving approach to problems in relationships is still at an early stage of development. It has not made an impact yet in politics, industrial relations or law. It is only in recent years that problem-solving conflict resolution has become a taught subject, and even now it is usually confined to a post-graduate level.

To go one step further and to eliminate structures and policies which generate conflict, violence and crime it would be necessary to go back to face-to-face societies in which there was no separation of those who determined the social norms and those who were required to observe them. Societies would need to be transformed from centralized systems, top-down administrations, to decentralized, bottom-up decision-making, if more face-to-face relationships were to be introduced. The views put forward by writers such as John Dryzek in his *Discursive Democracy* and Jane Mansbridge in her *Beyond Adversary Democracy*, and others referred to in the previous chapter, cannot be brushed aside. But a return to face-to-face societies is no longer possible. There have to be central authorities and perhaps even global authorities. However, the two are not necessarily incompatible. Bottom-up decision-making, reflecting human needs, is possible at a community level to deal with problems which occur at that level. From representatives at that level there can be an important input into central decision-making to bring macro decision-making into line with human needs.

Civilizations are now being forced to make a major decision. The evolution of the industrialized nation-state and trends towards a global economy with policies determined by the relatively powerful have tended to eliminate an important input from community levels. Deregulation trends in developed capitalist economies are still moving in that direction. Societies must now decide whether to allow natural evolution based on competition and relative power to determine the future, leading to more highly organized conflict, violence and crime, or to take control of evolution and to accommodate the basic drives and needs of the human race. In practice, this means a decision whether to shift from the traditional power politics frame of decision-making, and from the management control of institutions, to a more consultative problem-solving one. It means moving towards democracies that are not based on power or majorities, but which are participatory throughout all institutions.

Notes

1   J. Galtung, 'A Structural Theory of Aggression', *Journal of Peace Research*, 1 (1964).
2   A. Maslow, *Towards a Psychology of Being* (Princeton NJ, Princeton Press, 1962).
3   S. Renshon, *Psychological Needs and Political Behavior: A Theory of Personality and Political Efficacy* (New York, Free Press, 1974).
4   J. Davies, *Human Nature in Politics: The Dynamics of Political Behavior* (New York, John Wiley, 1963).
5   P. Sites, *Control: The Basis of Social Order* (New York, Dunellen Publishers, 1973).
6   P. Sites, 'Needs as Analogues of Emotions', in John Burton, ed., *Conflict: Human Needs Theory* (New York, St Martin's Press and London, Macmillan, 1990).
7   K. Lederer, ed., *Human Needs* (Cambridge MA, Oelgeschlager, Gunn and Hain, 1980).
8   The four books in the Conflict Series are John Burton, *Conflict: Resolution and Provention*; John Burton, ed., *Conflict: Human Needs Theory*; John Burton and Frank Dukes, eds, *Conflict: Readings in Management and Resolution*; and John Burton and Frank Dukes, *Conflict: Practices in Management, Settlement and Resolution* (New York, St Martin's Press and London, Macmillan, 1990).
9   D. Prothrow-Smith with M. Weissman, *Deadly Consequences: How Violence is Destroying our Teenage Population and a Plan to Begin Solving the Problem* (New York, Harper Perennial, 1991).

5

Decision-making

We have dealt with the human dimension of our utopian frame, and with problems of structural violence. Now we turn to the sources of the structural problem.

Social structures are the result of decisions which reflect the interests, beliefs, values and norms of those making them, and to some degree those of others likely to be affected. Authorities, be they majority governments, dictators, industrial managers or teachers and parents, must rely to some extent on compliance strategies for decisions to be implemented. Some degree of resistance and 'structural violence' is likely to be an outcome. If, however, there is an accurate assessment of responses and adjustments in decision-making, consensus support makes compliance strategies less necessary and less damaging.

Assessing responses

We are led, therefore, into the field of decision-making. Likely responses to decisions are not readily determined. In the power frame, in which it is assumed that the threat of sufficient force will deter unacceptable behaviours, little importance has been attached to informed anticipation of responses, especially at the level of international relations, but also at other levels when non-legitimized authorities are in control. A particular example is where there are self-appointed military dictatorships. On the contrary, the discussions which would be required to obtain a reliable assessment of attitudes and responses are avoided for fear that they will be interpreted as a sign of uncertainty about intention.

The military and political leadership of Iraq assumed when it invaded Kuwait that the United States would not risk another Vietnam. The opposite was the reality. Risks were being taken quite deliberately to overcome the humiliation of Vietnam. On the US side, false assumptions were made about public support for military and political leaderships in Iraq. Another false assumption was that by amassing overwhelming forces the United States would so threaten Iraq that it would capitulate.

Even at the national level central authorities have difficulty in assessing accurately likely responses to policies, with changes in government resulting. The alienated 20 per cent in a society are not represented or not influential in the decision-making processes. Minorities, young people and those in poverty are likely to be the casualties of macro policies, especially financial and economic policies, leading to costly anti-social behaviours. Even at the community and family levels responses to decisions and reactions to compliance measures are difficult to anticipate.

If responses to proposed decisions could be anticipated by employing more informed decision-making processes, the costs and consequences of compliance strategies could be assessed before decisions were made, and adjustments could be made accordingly.

In recent decades important advances have been made in decision-making processes. It is only forty years or so since decision-making models were simple stimulus-response models. Perceived aggression stimulated the response of defence and preparation for offence. Within a power frame little more could be expected. With the introduction of modern weapons and the obviously increased civilian costs of warfare, there was an incentive for a more thoughtful approach. Wiener in 1950 published *The Human Use of Human Beings*.[1] He used the Greek term 'cybernetics', meaning 'steersman', to highlight the need to anticipate possible responses to decisions before decisions are taken, and to make adjustments accordingly. In 1963 Deutsch, in his *The Nerves of Government*,[2] took this thinking forward and modified greatly power political international relations studies. His model was the electronic device in an aircraft that enables the pilot to perceive a storm ahead and to alter course accordingly, then return to the previous flight path. This was not rejecting power theories. It was to make better use of power and without some of its costly mistakes.

Insights into decision-making processes have led management and diplomacy towards more professional bargaining and negotiation, but both are still in a relative power and compliance frame. If no agreement is reached, then it is back to direct confrontation. There are still few significant attempts to bring to the surface the human dimension – values attached to ethnicity, independence and other factors. An industrial relations dispute typically has a focus on wages. Rarely are there brought to the surface issues arising out of personal relationships between management and workers or the personal identity of workers.

Some US judges have begun to insist on 'Alternative Dispute Settlement' processes before parties appear before them. But this is mainly to save time and expense rather than to provide an opportunity for a more analytical approach. The focus is still on compensation and resource distribution, with little analysis of underlying motivations and feelings, sometimes with disastrous consequences. (With relevant training, however, the mediators involved could perform a role which courts cannot pursue and, in some cases, help to avoid court action or to provide insights for judges which would not otherwise be available.)

In practice it is difficult and usually impossible to make accurate assessments of responses to decisions in the absence of some direct communication with those who will be affected. Such interaction can provide far more reliable data on likely responses than is otherwise possible. Ideally decisions would be joint decisions after each side had fully analysed relationships. But at most social levels such direct exploration is taken as a sign of weakness and is usually avoided, especially at the international level.

This suggests the need for the intervention of a third party which, without publicity, can offer to decision-makers and those likely to be affected, an opportunity to interact in an analytical way. Having been invited, not having had to take an initiative, neither side shows any sign of weakness. Having redefined the relationship problem, realistic assessments of responses become possible and informed decision-making can take place.

In the 1960s there was innovative research by some scholars who were working in the area of international relations and were witnessing the defeat of great powers by small nations, and asking why. They sought to intervene in existing situations of high tension and conflict by inviting parties to analytical discussions which they facilitated. They moved into the industrial relations and interpersonal relations arena and argued the need for a different kind of decision-making, an analytical one assisted by a facilitator, which would help to bring to the surface those values and motivations which are deliberately hidden in a bargaining situation.[3]

These analytical processes are useful in helping to resolve a conflict, but they are even more importantly an essential part of decision-making, for unless there are informed assessments of responses decisions can be dysfunctional.[4]

The need for facilitated change

For reasons of stability and the sense of security it promotes, institutionalized relationships are valued. Trade unions value the industrial structures which enable them to negotiate with employers, even though this is an adversarial relationship. Separate workplace bargaining is a shift which is usually not acceptable. International trade and strategic agreements, especially those negotiated as a result of power bargaining, are treated as permanent and subject to enforcement.

No institutional structures, however, no matter how appropriate at any given point of time, can be appropriate indefinitely. Environmental, economic

43

and social conditions alter continuously, as do the means by which individuals and identity groups seek to pursue their needs. Consequently, there must be built into institutions means of adjustment that adapt to altered circumstances in a continuous way.

This is, of course, the justification of democratic processes: regular elections, freedom of speech and publication, and others. In practice, however, such processes do not necessarily lead to the adjustments that are required to meet the needs of constituents. Within the so-called democratic system a government in office can readily make fundamental changes in policy and in structures. But a government in office may represent only certain interests and the changes may be opposed by more than 50 per cent of the public.

Nor do really democratic processes of change usually exist in public and private institutions. For example, while the need for regular consultation and adjustments in industrial management is recognized in management studies, it is only rarely that in practice there is any built-in mechanism by which adjustments are made that reflect the needs of all concerned. There are adjustments made as the consequence of protests and strikes, but rarely are there continuous processes of agreed change.

It is not sufficient for change to be continuous in response to altering conditions and perceptions. While dealing with an immediate problem is administratively and socially important, anticipation and proventive problem-solving is even more important in decision-making. It is the avoidance of problems in relationships that needs to be pursued, not just the making of adjustments after a problem has emerged. It follows that built-in decision-making processes of reassessment are required if conflict is to be avoided.

Problem-solving as an adjustment process

Analysing institutional processes and determining what adjustments might be required in an institution is a challenging enterprise. Analysis requires a problem-solving process, not the adversarial party political, or the industrial and international negotiating and bargaining ones which are traditional.

Problem-solving, in the sense of getting to the sources or causes of institutional or social-political problems, is, as has been suggested, a recent concept. Its more traditional and usual meaning in a political-social context is 'dealing with' by law enforcement or suppression. 'Peace-keeping' and 'peace-making' are of this nature. So, also, is power bargaining, which merely defers conflict rather than resolving any problem. The widespread process of 'mediation' is also within a power frame, the mediator seeking a compromise acceptable to the more powerful party. While these processes may be relevant to disputes involving negotiable material issues, they are not, as has been observed, appropriate when there are non-negotiable behavioural elements involved. A practical problem is that it is never clear whether a seeming dispute has or has not conflict components, requiring a mediator in a bargaining situation to have included in training an awareness of the nature of conflicts.

The new meaning of problem-solving, getting to the roots of a problem, implies a searching analysis by all those concerned in the light of which an agreement can be reached without any compromise of human needs. Rarely do bargaining processes accomplish this. Relationships remain which are potentially conflictual. (The steps to be taken to ensure that this analysis takes place without the introduction of power bargaining have been set out in explanatory detail in an appendix to *Conflict: Practices in Management, Settlement and Resolution* and in *Conflict Resolution: Its Language and Processes*.[5])

Not only does such an analysis direct attention to alternative policies and to structural changes which might be necessary. It also enables the parties, especially the parties which perceive themselves to be the more powerful, to make an accurate costing of the consequences of pursuing existing policies. Both those who might seek change and those who might seek to resist change are able to perceive directly the motives, concerns, dedication and needs of the other side. This costing is an important first step in arriving at agreement when parties are considering structural change.

The need for facilitation

Reference has been made to facilitation and facilitators. Within a behavioural frame, problem-solving conflict-resolution and conflict-provention processes are deeply analytical of behavioural responses to institutional and social norms. The analysis is carried out by the parties involved. It is unlikely, however, that such analyses can be accomplished without the assistance of facilitators. Their role is to direct attention to underlying behavioural elements that do not normally surface when parties in conflict meet face-to-face. They ensure a focus on the hidden issues giving rise to the problem and to the real costs of not adjusting to them. It is most unlikely that such an analytical process could be conducted within an institution, especially within an institutional frame that is adversarial in character, without the help of such a third party.

The role of the facilitator is not that of a mediator; resolution, not compromise, is sought. The United States Institute of Peace, a body financed directly by the Government, in 1994 commissioned a survey of organizations and individuals engaged in education, training and research in international conflict resolution. It argued that 'As ethnic, religious and regional conflicts emerge as perhaps the greatest challenge to peace in the post-Cold War era, conflict resolution skills training is in high demand.'

Facilitation is a professional role for which a great deal of training is required, not the few days that sometimes provide mediation skills. It is not training in process mainly, but a broad education in the nature of human relationships. Indeed, it is a serious mistake to seek a resolution of a deep-seated problem with no skills other than that of mediation or of applying general goodwill. Knowing what questions to ask, delving into the problem, requires a thorough knowledge of conflict in all its aspects.

Facilitation is a most active role. It is, however, never an authoritative role. The facilitator, or team of facilitators, is there to question in order to help analysis by the parties, not to act as judge applying norms or values. If this were to be done it would be perceived by the parties as taking sides in this analytical and no-fault setting.

It has been stressed that human needs such as needs of recognition and identity are not negotiable. But learning through direct communication that the other side has such needs, and learning also of the different ways in which it pursues them, starts the costing process. Consideration of options can then lead to the discovery and discussion of agreed behaviours.

Such analytical processes must frequently be informal and even secret so that there can be exploration without commitment until agreement is reached. This is particularly the case when leaderships and party political conditions have to be met. Talking to the 'enemy' and changes in policies are usually not possible in party political circumstances. Consequently, facilitators and scholars pursuing these activities frequently do not feel free to give publicity to their work while it is in process. Indeed, later publicity of a particular case can be damaging to the process because parties to future facilitation could fear the possibilities of publicity. The same principles apply at industrial, social and family levels also.

Theorizing or realism?

The problem-solving approach assumes that peoples and leaderships have the decision-making ability to take charge of the present and future rather than to leave developments to accidental or evolutionary power processes. It also assumes that even highly organized and powerful interest groups would be prepared to look beyond their immediate interests, and enter into analytically based decision-making calculated to satisfy present and future social needs rather than just immediate interests. These assumptions imply that societies, having gone through many forms of feudalism, may finally be approaching a stage at which the traditionally influential are sufficiently insecure and fearful of the future that they would be prepared to join in such an analytical process and be part of a political consensus.

This may not be as unrealistic as it may seem. A shift from one interest or value oriented ideology to another does not offer any solution on which there can be a consensus. There would be, therefore, no inducement for the privileged to give up present advantages, or for the underprivileged to refrain from protest responses and, if perceived necessary, from violence. But an analytical and problem-solving process offers a different option. Unlike an ideological solution which has to be imposed on those with different ideologies, an analytical process leads to a consideration of decision-making options that can be implemented only when there is a consensus. One of the lessons of history is that change that is to be stable cannot be imposed, it must be based on consensus and consent. In a climate of conflict, violence and crime, there are reasons for accuracy in decision-making.

However, reliable decision-making reassessments of structures and policies must involve all concerned. Facilitated conflict provention and resolution, and decision-making generally, becomes less and less practicable as decision-making becomes more centralized and more remote. It could reasonably be argued that recent discoveries in facilitated conflict resolution were in the past a part of practice in face-to-face tribal societies in which all members were aware of all behavioural aspects of problems. This lends support to the view that far more community-based solving of social problems is desirable.

Such is the utopian frame in which we now discuss, in Part Two, the adversarial institutions which are the foundation of modern societies.

Notes

1   N. Wiener, *The Human Use of Human Beings* (New York, Eyre and Spottiswoode, 1950).
2   K. Deutsch, *The Nerves of Government* (New York, Free Press, 1963).
3   J. Burton, *Deviance, Terrorism and War: The Processes of Solving Unsolved Social and Political Problems* (New York, St Martin's Press and London, Macmillan, 1979).
4   J. Burton, *Conflict and Communication* (London, Macmillan, 1969).
5   J. Burton and F. Dukes, *Conflict: Practices in Management, Settlement and Resolution* (New York, St Martin's Press and London, Macmillan, 1990); J. Burton, *Conflict Resolution: Its Language and Processes* (Lanham MD, Scarecrow Press, 1996).

Part Two

From compulsion to consent

Within the behavioural decision-making frame we now examine the main institutions of a society: the family, leaderships, decision-making institutions, administrations which carry out decisions, the workplace, the legal system, and also the global environment in which decisions are made.

The conceptualization of the institutions that would evolve within this frame, which is the subject of this Part, is not difficult. The practical problem is to find the specific changes which would be required in existing institutions. Suggestions are made under each of the institutional headings. These are all fairly superficial. What is really required is applied research in each field carried out within the context of the totality of systems, and by those in a system who know the problems and the possibilities. And this needs to be a continuing process. This Part is designed to define the problem area, to challenge conventional wisdom and to stimulate thought.

6

The family

As has been argued, an analysis of conflict, violence and crime made within a power or compliance frame is not primarily concerned with human behaviour. In that frame the assumption is that the person is malleable and, therefore, is susceptible to compliance processes. Accordingly, non-compliance is attributed to deliberate anti-social behaviours or abnormalities which require deterrent punishments or psychological and medical treatments.

Once the assumption of malleability is questioned, a human factor is introduced into any analysis of the sources of conflict, violence and crime. It is this human element which makes possible a holistic approach and an analysis which explains non-compliant behaviours in all institutions at all social levels.

The family, being the environment in which relationship norms are first learned, could reasonably be regarded as the most influential institution in societies. Different cultural and religious communities, for example Christians and Jews, can interact over several thousand years and still retain their separate belief systems, suggesting a persistent early learning process. Childhood experiences must inevitably affect the characters and behaviours of all adults, including, of course, those who in adulthood become involved in public institutions including leaderships, legislatures, public services, industrial relations, legal processes and relations between ethnic groups and nations. These institutions are probably adversarial for evolutionary reasons. Being adversarial they would attract those who tend to be adversarial in their personal relationships, thus accentuating confrontational processes. The family has its own compliance processes, sometimes taking extreme forms including violence. For the same human needs reasons these are resisted just as they are in society generally. Is there a significant contribution made by the family to the adversarial nature of public institutions? Could this influence be controlled, could public institutions be made less rather than more adversarial by alterations in family norms and practices?

The family: a private institution

The family is not usually featured in analyses of political and social problems which societies experience because the family is traditionally regarded as a private, not a public institution and, therefore, not relevant in political analysis. It is not socially acceptable to attribute aggressive individual leadership or management behaviours to early experiences. Curricula vitae do not include accounts of early experiences even though these may determine personalities and capabilities even more than university educations, which are documented. Inquiries by prospective employers or voters into family experiences would reasonably be regarded as an infringement of privacy.

Even known violent behaviours within the family are not regarded as being subject to public scrutiny. As Richard Gelles observes, ' "Selective inattention" is a useful way of characterizing research on violence in the family.'[1] It is still only the unusual cases of violence which come to public attention. What takes place in the family is treated in modern societies as private to the extent that officials who have responsibility for dealing with violence and crime have no right of entry into the household; social workers and teachers who become aware of physical abuse do not feel free to make reports to officials; and neighbours tend to respect rights of privacy which they also value. Despite publicity given to family and related crimes (see below), observation of privacy still dominates.

Indeed, one hesitates to include this sensitive issue of the family in a political analysis for fear that the reader will immediately associate the concern with some special religious value or ideological orientation. In a holistic approach, however, the family must be acknowledged as an institution which, along with others, requires analysis.

While there is a great deal of empirical data available on tensions and violence in the family, there is little known about the degree of influence which family experiences have on behaviours later in life. In the absence of extensive statistical analyses, which are urgently required, only deductive conclusions can be reached about the effect of family problems on the later personalities and behaviours of people. However, the data available strongly suggests that deductive reasoning and hypotheses would be valid.

The changing structure of the family

The nuclear family, parents and children, is an ever-changing institution. In tribal societies it was generally merged into the whole and child-care was a social responsibility. Furthermore, the family and children were brought up within a community in which the members knew each other, in which it was socially unacceptable to continue hostilities, and in which, therefore, reconciliation rather than punishment was the means of dealing with problems in relationships.[2] Alienation was not a normal experience. Children did not leave home!

In early agricultural conditions, by contrast, the nuclear family operated as an integrated work unit. This was within a wider agricultural society, but a less integrated community. The family as a work unit would have helped to some degree to avoid stress on family relationships and to promote the child-hood learning of social norms. Early forms of manufacturing, weaving, car-pentry and other such crafts were also home-based, the family acting again as a unit, though each member had specific roles.

With industrialization, however, in which there was a separate workplace for labourers, members of the family had separate roles. The mother tended to stay at home child-minding and undertaking household duties. The male, being the wage-earner and provider, emerged as the one in authority. It was at this point that problems of recognition and identity of the carer and house-keeper as a person emerged. The female began to experience a 'devalued sense of self' and resistance emerged, provoking violent responses.[3] By the seventeenth century in New England there was intervention into family af-fairs and violence was forbidden by law. Violence seemed to emerge as the male in due course experienced what a judge said was 'a threat to the offend-ers' identity'.[4] This revenge-type response has in recent years become ex-treme in many cases, such as when an estranged husband killed his former wife and nine others at a wedding reception for the former sister-in-law in April 1996 in Canada.

With further industrialization, workplace relationships spilled over into additional after-work social activities. Husbands and fathers were even more removed from wives and mothers, and a sense of inequality became the main issue for the latter.[5] There have been continuing trends in this direction, lead-ing to increases in separations with inevitable effects on child development. In contemporary conditions both parents frequently go out to work. Overtime is more frequent. In 1971 the US Department of Labor reported that married women accounted for 60 per cent of all women in work outside the home and over 40 per cent of all women worked. This would not always be from neces-sity, but, in many cases, as a means of acquiring a separate role and identity. These percentages have risen steadily ever since. In many communities the working father and the stay-at-home mother with at least two children is now the exception. Step-families are outnumbering the old traditional family.

Industries, and societies generally, are not yet coping with the consequent problem of child-care. An extra problem has emerged with an exponential increase in single-parent families, typically suffering poverty, especially when child-care makes outside work unfeasible. The linking of male partners who are not fathers of the family children has often led to extreme cases of stress and violence, including the murder of children, more usually by the partner, but sometimes by the mother.

More children are killed by family violence than die through car accidents, drowning and other such mishaps. Clearly, the number of children who suffer at least some physical, emotional and mental damage as a result of family tensions would be far, far greater than the number of homicides. Limited surveys do not reveal the extent of the problem, but evidence mounts. Responses from Australian primary school students show a widespread sense of 'familylessness' and anxieties over parental fighting.[6]

The patterns of control experienced in the family situation, including male dominance and compliance measures, tend to become the norm when those who have had the experience themselves are in a position of authority. This is inevitable when the same norms are widely observed. The same compliance culture influences the way in which children are educated in schools.

The weakened nuclear family leads to other abuses of children which must have long-term effects. In 1996 a Royal Commission conducted in Sydney, Australia, an investigation into the paedophilial activities of the clergy, leading businessmen, bureaucrats responsible for the caring of children, police, teachers and families. It was found that the majority of victims were boys, frequently as young as ten or so, who had left home because of violence there, and who took advantage of opportunities for better living conditions. At that age 'the boys became totally desensitised. They felt that they had no value as human beings and, therefore, no one else had any value.'[7] Evidence given revealed that boys in care were subjected to rape and mistreatments of many kinds, with lasting social effects. Apparently 'selective inattention' goes far beyond the privacy of the family, but for the same reasons. It was interesting that, once made public, these issues attracted a lot of public attention and, decades after, are leading to claims for damages against individuals and the government. No doubt a similar investigation would reveal the same age groups and numbers of girls leaving home and seeking means of living elsewhere, and being abused by their carers.

A Royal Commission is merely an investigation into certain types of behaviour. It does not seek explanations. Similarly, war crimes trials are for purposes of punishment, not explanation. Until there is explanation there can be no provention (getting to the sources of problems), only ineffective prevention. Punishing Nazi war criminals did not deter Bosnian war criminals. The problem goes far deeper, perhaps to the revenge behaviours which are known to be stimulated by violence and coercion experienced in early life. Is the modern family as an institution responsible to any significant degree for violent and criminal behaviours in society, and for increased adversarial behaviours in public institutions?

Currently there are frequent reports of mass killings in ethnic conflicts on the instructions of self-appointed leaderships. There are war crimes trials as a result. But this mass killing is condemned only in extreme cases and when conducted by non-governmental military leaders. 'Great powers' and those in the field of power politics strategies accept civilian killing, even nuclear mass killing, as inevitable parts of 'just wars', these being defined as wars in the pursuit of national interests. To separate such behaviours from more local serial killings, murders and domestic violence, or indeed from less dramatic adversarial and aggressive behaviours in politics and industry, is to make quite artificial distinctions. They are all in the power frame in which any threatening opposition is dehumanized.

The continuum becomes clear when specific conflict situations are examined. Typically protest against some unacceptable structural condition, as exists in Northern Ireland, Israel, Sri Lanka and many other countries, commences with ordinary political protest processes, then escalates towards more public forms such as parades which lead to conflict with police seeking to contain them, then step-by-step to organized military confrontations and terrorism in many forms. In due course there may be 'ethnic cleansing'.

Separating these different levels and forms of violence into special categories is an extension of specialization in the social sciences according to social levels. It eliminates consideration of commonalities and a holistic approach to an analysis of the sources of problems in each specialization. The alternative strategy of acknowledging human attributes and needs and seeking processes of resolution does not emerge in this perception of violence.

Despite an increased interest in the family, the tendency of problems in the family to spill over into society in general has been largely ignored in social sciences and in policies, even though a great deal of conflict, violence and crime at all social levels and at the international level can probably be traced to the family and to early childhood. The probability is there because it can be assumed that there are in families many instances of aggressive and even violent compliance strategies leading to alienation, feelings of revenge and learned power orientations which affect behaviours later in life. But it has to be observed that this is merely deductive or inferential thinking. There is still little known about the influence of the family on behaviours in other institutions.

The social costs of family violence

Whether or not it is relevant to the problem of adversarial institutions, the family continues to create expensive social problems of conflict, violence and crime. Gaol, hospital and caring costs alone would justify large sums being spent on provention by the education of men and women with family responsibilities and by social work interventions into family relationships.

In some quarters there is an increasing concern over this problem of childcare and development. David Hamburg has, as President of the Carnegie Foundation, devoted time and resources to its study, pointing to the lack of development opportunities children are getting in the home – television being their main source of information. He recommends financial assistance to single-parent families in need, prenatal care and education, local services, the identification of women likely to be under stress because of the needs of work, continuing post-natal care and education.[8] Family relationships and child-rearing are probably not just the most important activities in any society, but also the most difficult. The assumption that there are inherent human abilities which allow parents to take care of children is false for structural conditions are constantly changing, parents lack models and training, and adjustments are constantly required. The main adjustments children have to make in entering adult life are at stages at which they are resisting pressures to observe family norms. Education on the nature of relationships, sex and society generally, and on ways in which to handle differences in viewpoints, needs to be ongoing from schools through to post-graduate levels. The present stage of change in which the male can no longer expect to maintain his traditional dominant position in the family and in social organizations may make education easier. But as yet people qualified to instruct are rarely available. Perhaps approaches to social studies based on the assumption of the primacy of human needs of recognition and identity would help to provide the required frame.

Besides education and counselling, thought needs to be given to structural changes in the family. There are some cultures which seem to have avoided some of these problems. In Israel there are collective settlements (*kibbutzim*) in which the family is subordinate and child-care is a high priority, and co-operative settlements (*moshavim*) which are kinship centres. Chinese culture seems to give a high priority to child-care and development. One means has been multiple mothering in child centres.[9] These all point to the need for a questioning of the Western-style nuclear family as being sacrosanct.

Perhaps the single-parent family should be given the opportunity to live within a kibbutz-type community, rather than merely receiving some financial support to remain at home, alienated and without a social role. This would make it possible for mothers to seek work, while at the same time providing children with needed relationships and development opportunities. Same-sex parent families also need relevant structures so that children will not feel alienated later in life, becoming a misfit in one form or another. Different societies have different options and all need to be explored.

Being more open about family problems, and in particular making public the possible connection between family experiences and revenge-type behaviours in public institutions, could have the effect of stimulating an awareness by adults of their own personality problems, leading to self-imposed constraints.

Given a privacy requirement, the means of bringing family problems into the open is probably by some form of neighbourhood watch, perhaps the appointment by a neighbourhood community of an independent social worker who would not be caught up in local controversies, preferably paid by community members so that there is no outside interference. This could lead to a consensus concerning opportunities for professional entry into households and to proventive activities.

The progression to adulthood

No survey of the family as an influence on public institutions and policies is complete without taking into account 'adopted families', such as street gangs and other support groups which assist teenagers in their quest for identity and development.

Where there has been family success, emerging into the wider society as a developed person with a social role and identity need not be a major problem for young people. Such a person is likely to play a part in a public institution, but it is not likely to be an aggressive one. Further development takes place in a supportive environment, but it is an adversarial one and is preparation for aggressive leadership roles and adversarial behaviours in adversarial institutions.

Where, however, the young person feels alienated, or maybe leaves the family home in search of further development and identity, aggressive behaviours are likely. A street gang provides 'rituals marking their passage to manhood'.[10]

There are few countries in the world in which there is as much community violence as in South Africa. There are also few countries in which there are more insights and constructive responses by those who seek to address the problem. Community organization and conciliation processes are slowly taking the place of the Western justice system.[11] Community organization is important as a means of providing continuing support after the family is no longer sufficient, or when the family has failed in its purposes. Even dreaded street gangs make their contribution when young people are still seeking their identity and role in society in conditions in which traditional institutions have failed them.

Notes

1 R. Gelles, *The Violent Home: A Study of Physical Aggression between Husbands and Wives* (Beverly Hills CA, Sage Publications, 1972).
2 S. Rugege, 'Conflict Resolution', *Track Two* (Rondebosch, Journal of the Centre for Conflict Resolution), 5: 1 (March 1996), p. 23.
3 See Gelles, *The Violent Home*, p. 187.
4 Ibid.
5 P. Stein, J. Richman and N. Hannon, *The Family: Functions, Conflicts and Symbols* (Menlo Park CA, Addison Wesley, 1977).
6 *Canberra Times* (5 April 1996), p. 8.
7 Reports on Royal Commission, *The Australian* (April 1996).

8   D. Hamburg MD, *Today's Children: Creating a Future for a Generation in Crisis* (New York, Times Books, Random House, 1992).
9   Stein *et al.*, *The Family*.
10 D. Pinnock, 'Gangs, Guns and Rites of Passage', *Track Two*, 5: 1 (March 1996), p. 10.
11 D. Omar, 'And Justice for All', *Track Two*, 5: 1 (March 1996), pp. 4–6.

7

Leaderships

Leadership problems

Problems with leaderships are a recognized part of history. They are universal. They frequently have damaging effects in all systems and at all social
levels. It could reasonably be argued that the major problems of modern societies (and it may have been true throughout history) are problems associated
with acquiring and maintaining leadership roles. From the family to the nation, struggles to acquire and to maintain leadership in societies are a major
source of strife.

The previous chapter on the family sought to suggest that the problem of
leadership was deeply embedded in the evolution of societies and of the nuclear family in particular. For this reason the problems of leadership have
been an accepted part of political and social systems and organizations. So
much has this been the case that until three or so decades ago there were few
studies of the problem. In a well-researched book, *The Scientific Study of Political Leadership*, Glenn Paige has shown that leadership was not a subject for
such discussion until the 1950s.[1] In the *American Political Science Review*, of
the 2,614 articles published in the first fifty-seven years, only seventeen included 'leader' or 'leadership' in their titles. He observes that his own book
Political Leadership would have been classified by the Library of Congress as
HM14I, signifying 'the great man, leadership, prestige, cf. genius': no sugges-
tion of problems with leaderships.

Even when leadership problems became a subject of interest, the bulk of
works were on leadership attributes, drawing very much from the history of
leadership. In 1961 Stephen Graubard and Gerald Holton edited *Excellence
and Leadership in a Democracy*.[2] There were twelve articles, all dwelling on the
positive aspects of leadership and strongly advancing the view that the role of
leadership was to convince followers. A leader's job was to ask for and to
obtain power.

More recently there have been revelations about leaders who have been ill,
sometimes mentally incapable of carrying out their role, and the way in which
this has been covered up, signifying once again the traditions that govern

leadership-respect, regardless of quality.[3]

This glorification of excellence in leadership (the acquisition and use of power) and the traditional absence of an interest in problems of leadership corresponds with the traditional absence of any interest in human behaviours and decision-making. Within a power frame this is to be expected. If human behaviour is assumed to be malleable, then excellence in leadership is in obtaining power and exercising it with strength and determination whether or not it is obtained by consensus processes. If there is no institutional frame in which problems can be resolved (and by definition the power frame lacks one), then competitive power politics is the means. This invites aggressive leaderships and temporary admiration of them.

For example, post-First World War settlements and the Great Depression of the 1930s brought Hitler into power in Germany. There were widely felt needs for strong leadership to overcome problems faced by the nation. In such stress situations 'strong' leaders receive wide support. If there had not been Hitler there would have been another ambitious leader coming to the fore. Leadership struggles are an expected and accepted part of modern political processes. And this applies at all social levels.

We know from experience that leadership in the power system cannot, even with the best of personal intentions, contribute to problem-solving. It is a sign of weakness to admit failure, to adjust ideas to those of others and to alter a policy. Leaders must be aggressive when on the defensive. We have examples of leaders seeking to improve their popular standing by aggressive behaviours against other nations, even expensive wars.

Nor can leadership in the power system provide continuity in policy. Societies comprise different and sometimes incompatible interest and ideological communities. Widespread acceptability is unlikely for any leaderships that seem to favour some interest groups more than others. It follows that there cannot be a continuing acceptability in the competitive political party system, or, indeed, in any power system. This invites defensive measures to offset unacceptability.

Leadership and needs satisfaction

Individuals seek satisfaction for themselves directly and, also, indirectly through identity groups, be they football teams, ethnic communities or adversarial party politics. The individual struggle for a leadership role frequently reflects this same frustration and need for personal recognition and identity. The warlord and dictatorship phenomena are evidence of this. Going back into the life of such people reveals their earlier social problems.

We have argued that the pursuit of human needs requires societies to adjust institutions to human behaviours so that there can be development without anti-social and violent consequences. Such consequences, however, are not confined to illegal behaviours such as robbery and assault. They include many behaviours that are legal, from physically damaging competitive sports to adversarial political behaviours. They are all means of pursuing goals of recognition and identity. Treating leadership problems as separate from other problems associated with human behaviours is ignoring the fundamental issues that require attention.

It could be deduced that people who have experienced security, who have achieved identity through social, professional or institutional success, would enact leadership roles quite differently from those who use a leadership role for their own needs pursuit purposes. Empirically this seems to be the case. The wartime British leader of the Opposition, Clement Atlee, was able to work with Prime Minister Winston Churchill during the Second World War, despite different political philosophies. Later Atlee enacted what was very much a facilitating role in the post-war period when he became Prime Minister. In Australia there were leaders of this kind, for example Ben Chifley, who during the Second World War and after was a very secure person despite a humble background. On the other hand, there have been leaders in both countries who were typically aggressive and dictatorial in their manner, reflecting in all cases personal insecurities.

While all kinds of personalities are attracted to leadership roles, some for reasons of personal ambition, some for altruistic reasons, the nature of traditional power-political leadership roles tends to attract those who have personal goals to fulfil. This is saying no more than that there are personality problems in leaders as there are amongst peoples in societies generally. The leadership role, however, has far greater potential for either constructive or destructive outcomes than any other. There are in some systems checks and balances that are intended to help avoid leadership problems. There is a need in all systems, not for specific restraints or controls, for these can be challenged, but for constitutions, institutions and processes that make such problem behaviours irrelevant.

The legitimacy problem

The question of legitimacy has been a core issue in discussions of leaderships. As observed above, the traditional view has been that leadership 'excellence' consists of winning approval to exercise power in decision-making. There are many ways of doing this, from personal persuasion to a popularly accepted military coup. Legitimacy in a problem-solving frame would be defined differently.

Legitimacy or acceptability is a relative term: it is measured by the degree of popular support from those over whom authority is exercised. In practice, leaderships can be legal and in this sense legitimized, but lack acceptability. They can also be accepted but lack legitimacy, as in the case of a popular military coup. In practice, support is more important than legality. Support can pave the way for changes in constitutions and, therefore, in legality, when necessary.

Hence we have an interplay between human characteristics and political circumstances. May it not be that the traditional social and political power system attracts certain types of persons and also determines leadership behaviours? If this is the case, altered institutions and processes might equally condition alternative leadership behaviours.

There is, however, another element that could be more important for societies than legitimacy. Dictionaries give many meanings to legitimacy. One is that which is 'based on correct or acceptable principles of reasoning'. Such a definition applied to leadership authorities raises some challenging issues. Would a military dictatorship which had little popular support, but which pursued policies which were based on acceptable principles of reasoning, be legitimate? Rephrased, are leaderships that look ahead in terms of community interests 'legitimate' even though they act in ways that do not have immediate popular support?

Implied in the question is one that is most challenging to notions of democracy. Are we bound to have authorities that play to popular opinion, or can we include within the notion of democracy those authorities who defy popular opinion in order to act in what they consider to be the longer-term interests of society, including the interests of future generations?

In the party political system, a government once in office can pursue policies that may not have popular support. In the absence of popular support legitimacy rests wholly on legality. In due course, faced with an election, such a government must either change its policies, persuade the electorate or risk defeat. In this sense the democratic system based on popular support has a serious weakness: principle and 'reasoning' must give place to support.

Dictatorships would argue that leadership which lacks popular support is sometimes inevitable and even desirable. It could be that some dictators could be legitimized leaders in the sense that their power base could enable them to look to the longer-term rather than just to the immediate interests of those whom they lead. Dictatorships, by implication, would hold the view that legitimization is a function of performance judged by standards of leadership rather than by legality and the measure of popular support. This assumes an individual or small group ability to determine goals and policies without input from those affected.

Dictatorships are extreme cases. The same assumption is made by democratically elected party-political leaders. The adversarial decision-making processes which govern modern democratic systems are based on the same assumption: that decision-making is democratic and legitimized even without inputs from those affected.

Standards of assessment

In the absence of any universally agreed goals of organizations and societies, there can be only ideological and subjective assessments of legitimization. Each would-be leader has his or her own preconceived notions. There being little reasoned discussion aimed at agreement amongst rival leaderships, power confrontations in one form or another inevitably determine legitimacy.

The West's standards for assessing leaderships are related to types of systems rather than the quality of leadership. Foreign leaderships, no matter how unpopular, are tolerated by major powers if they operate within 'democracies' and observe free market mechanisms, while leaderships in dictatorships that do not support the free market are opposed, no matter how popular.

But standards by which to assess leaderships cannot reasonably rest on types of economic systems or levels of response to the electorate. Take, as an example, a long-term problem that decision-makers face, such as population or the environment. Problems in these areas are not tackled largely because few leaders in any system can afford politically to place longer-term goals, of little election interest to most members of the public, before the immediate and strong interests of those who resist population controls or destroy the environment. As another example, a political candidate who runs on a platform that promises tax reductions is far more likely to be elected than one who advocates ecological reform or more education and health services, implying increased taxes to pay for them. The reality is that within so-called 'democratic' systems, at least as we now know them, a far-sighted leadership is probably impossible. Military or other dictatorships, with their precarious hold on the populace, are no better off. Both must finally rely on the support of powerful special interests.

Leadership in a behavioural frame

The traditional concept of leadership, developed within the political power frame, is in practice quite incompatible with concepts of consensus democracy, and incompatible, also, with problem-solving approaches to policies. What needs to be considered is not the character of leaderships and their behaviours within the traditional power political system, but the nature and role of leadership in a problem-solving frame.

In a problem-solving frame the role of leadership in decision-making is essentially the role of a problem-solving facilitator. It is to promote analytical discussion of a problem, taking into account varying perceptions and interpretations, and to help deduce appropriate policies. It is to direct attention to longer-term costs and consequences of alternative policies. Such leadership would seek to ensure that all available knowledge is employed in defining and dealing with problems. Asking the appropriate questions, ensuring that data is not hidden, questioning assumptions, encouraging analysis and exploring alternative viewpoints, are all part of this role.

There is implied, clearly, an unusual ability to adopt a holistic perspective, to ask the penetrating questions and to help in deducing options. Reich in *The Work of Nations* describes the role of those who seek to deal with major problems in business relationships:

> Thus one of the strategic broker's tasks is to create settings in which problem-solvers and problem-identifiers can work together without undue interference. The strategic broker is a facilitator and a coach – finding the people in both camps who can learn most from one another, giving them whatever resources they need, letting them go at it long enough to discover new complements between technologies and customer needs, but also providing them with enough guidance so that they don't lose sight of mundane goals like earning a profit.[4]

In a problem-solving, problem-avoiding society, this is the kind of person required in leadership at all levels, from the family and school, to industry and government.

Both democratic and authoritarian systems, as they exist today, are power systems. In both cases there is an authority that is free to make decisions and to implement decisions to the degree that it has political power. If societies sought leaderships which could act as facilitators in resolving problems, there would have to be a move away from systems in which decisions are made to satisfy pressure groups and to win popular support, and away from systems in which majority interests can disregard minorities and the less powerful. Societies would have to move towards systems in which decisions were made on the basis of an informed consensus, leading to consent, about means of dealing with current and anticipated problems.

This means that an essential quality of leadership in a problem-solving frame is more than an ability just to respond to demands, pressures, interests and the views of an electorate. It is an ability to help in defining the goals of the electorate and to arrive at a consensus on policies designed to satisfy the needs of societies, not only now but also in the longer term. Ideal leadership, in other words, is neither just a response to those led, nor an imposition of preconceived convictions. Ideal leadership requires insights, imagination and creativity; an ability to foresee and to prevent, as well as to resolve problems rather than to handle confrontations; and, also, a flair for communication.

System influences on leadership types

The kind of leadership a society requires can never be a personal phenomenon. No one person can have all the necessary knowledge and qualifications for leadership. So the concept of leadership must include processes whereby there is consultation that ensures the bringing together of all interests and all available knowledge into an interactive decision-making setting. The 'leader' in such a process is a facilitator.

For such a leader to achieve the role, the election process would require political campaigns that were based on advocacy of processes by which policies were determined, rather than on specific policies designed to attract votes. In some countries, for example Australia, there are in legislatures groups of independents and small minorities who are concerned with the decision-making process rather than with specific policies, these being open for debate. Probably it is only such a focus than can break down the adversarial nature of party political politics, industrial relations, legal processes and social relationships generally, and make possible facilitators as leaders.

This is suggesting that *the processes by which policies are arrived at, rather than the policies finally agreed upon, would be the main concern of a non-adversarial system*. This raises an interesting political question: would a political party attract electoral support if its platform were confined to a spelling-out of problem-solving processes rather than based on specific policies? If such a platform were to be accepted by an electorate, there would be no role for separate political parties as the sponsors of candidates.

An alternative frame

In all relationships there are problems to be resolved. They probably cannot be resolved within parts of the system, for example within one particular institution. Relationships are affected by the total social environment, including the family, education, health, housing, conditions of employment and almost every social condition experienced by members of the society. If there is power domination in one part of a system, this will affect others. If there is to be a legitimization of authorities in societies, then it must be of all authorities. In short, a shift from power to problem-solving can be practical only if it takes place throughout the whole system, from personal and family relationships, through work relationships, to relationships with authorities.

This implies procedures and processes in decision-making quite different from the traditional ones. It means that at the national level there would be genuine analytical discussions, not party political stances. It means there would be informed and educated advisers who had adequate experience in consultative decision-making and problem-solving in addition to their professional field. It would mean a media and public aware of the nature of problem-solving and the need for a facilitator as leader.

This is not necessarily only a dream. People in most democracies are fed up with party political positions and an absence of meaningful dialogue. They could respond positively to an alternative approach. When the longer-term costs and consequences of inequalities, and of injustices that reflect influence and power, become a social concern, support for an alternative decision-making process is a political and social possibility.

The nature of this alternative decision-making process is already suggested by the concept of problem-solving conflict resolution. It requires decision-makers who can define, articulate and pursue a policy in the context of human needs and responses. For this to be possible there has to be direct communication by decision-makers with peoples who suffer the structural violence that are the source of problems. Decision-makers must have the means of assessing the costs and consequences of policies that threaten the recognition and development of those affected. This means a thorough understanding of human needs, and the way in which they are extensively frustrated from early childhood to life at the workplace and socially.

It can be seen, therefore, that the leadership problem, the cause of so much domestic and international strife, is unsolvable without major changes in the decision-making institutions in which leaders operate. One way forward, therefore, would be adjustment of political, industrial and social institutions so that they require decision-making to be problem-solving and leaders to be facilitators. So we now turn to legislatures.

Notes

1   G. Paige, *The Scientific Study of Political Leadership* (New York, Free Press, 1977).
2   S. Graubard and G. Holton, *Excellence and Leadership in a Democracy* (New York, Columbia University Press, 1961).
3   J. Post and R. Robins, *When Illness Strikes the Leader: The Dilemma of the Captive King* (New Haven CT, Yale University Press, 1993).
4   R. Reich, *The Work of Nations* (New York, Vintage Press, 1992).

8

Legislatures

It is legislatures that are looked to in democratic societies to bring about the changes needed to deal with problems. It is legislatures that are expected to take care of any social problems that the free market arm of democracy might create. That this is the role of legislatures, and that they have, as democratically elected bodies, the necessary legitimacy and capability, is the common ideological foundation of modern democracies.

This view requires a searching examination, regardless of traditional support. The reality is that modern democracies are failing in the areas of economic justice. Widespread conflict, violence and crime are realities. Why the failure? What changes are required to make legislatures both legitimate and capable of dealing with the immediate and longer-term problems of societies?

Adversarial legislatures

Traditional views are reflected in definitions. To quote *The New Columbia Encyclopedia*, a legislature is a

> representative assembly empowered to enact statute law. Generally the representatives who compose a legislature are constitutionally elected by a broad spectrum of the population. While rules of law have always been a concern for society, the use of legislatures for their establishment is a relatively modern phenomenon. In earlier times, human laws were considered part of the universal natural law, discoverable through the use of reason rather than made by the declaration of men. With the growth of belief in positive law, the increasing need in emerging modern society for adaptable law, and the decline of monarchical power, however, legislatures with law-making powers came about ... In its early history, the English Parliament ... consisted of representatives chosen according to classes or estates ... Out of the estates arose the typical bicameral system, in which an upper house represented the nobility and clergy and the lower house represented the bourgeoisie ...

An extension of this definition of a legislature would be a definition of democracy. The same encyclopedia, in defining 'democracy', asserts that:

> Such a philosophy places a high value on the equality of individuals and would free people as far as possible from restraints not self-imposed. It insists that necessary restraints be imposed only by the consent of the majority and that they conform to the principle of equality.

These definitions could be interpreted as implying that the past trends that led to wider representation and democratic decision-making processes are continuous, and that ultimately all citizens will be represented and their concerns addressed. But this would be a false interpretation. The definitions in fact reveal the limited nature of the traditional notion of representation, and the undemocratic nature of the majority rule decision-making process of legislatures.

Modern legislatures initially brought together the major interest groups of an evolving agricultural society, subsequently an industrial society. Different viewpoints found expression. But it was not then a concern that an underclass was being created and was excluded from the process. There has been little change over the years in this respect. On the contrary, the trend is probably in the other direction. Legislatures are becoming more and more influenced by organized interest groups, and are less and less catering to the concerns of those who are not so represented.

In many countries, while there may be the right to vote, only 50 per cent or so of the electorate do vote. This reflects a lack of identification with the system. In some countries, while voting may not be rigged in any illegal way, elections are run by party professionals who have experience in using polls, the media and local organizations to encourage their supporters to vote and to discourage others. Funding of elections also affects competitive outcomes. Within a party political system there is no commitment to universal representation.

As for majority rule decision-making, it could hardly be less democratic in the sense of taking into account and legislating to meet the requirements of all concerned. It could reasonably be argued that legislatures that would be democratic are not possible when legislative decisions are based on adversarial decision-making processes. Majority rule is very much within a power frame. Minority interests can be brushed aside.

In short, legislatures are, by origin and by consensus definition, adversarial in character. They rest on majority decision-making. The implication is that minorities will and can conform – an assumption that is no longer valid, if it ever was. Furthermore, legislatures are not wholly representative. This again implies that those who are outside this adversarial system will and can conform to decisions taken by others.

This becomes even clearer when a further extension of the concept of legislatures and democracy is made by examining a definition of ethnicity. In today's world ethnic groups are an inevitable component of most states, due to migrations and changes of boundaries resulting from wars. But the consensus concept reflected in the notion of ethnicity does not acknowledge a representation problem. An 'ethnic group' is defined merely as a 'distinct category in the population of the wider society'. Ethnocentrism has been regarded in this institutional frame as an extremist, even abnormal type of behaviour. Ethnocentrism is

> the feeling that one's group has a mode of living, values, and patterns of adaptation that are superior to other groups ... Violence, discrimination, proselytizing, and verbal aggressiveness are other means whereby ethnocentrism may be expressed.

This view of ethnocentrism reflects the traditional viewpoint that is promoted within a majority-dominated system. Within a behavioural frame, which hypothesizes inherent human needs of recognition and identity that *will* be pursued, ethnocentrism emerges as a natural, an inevitable response to denials of any other opportunities by which to secure recognition and identity. It requires for its treatment, not repression, but the provision of institutions and social norms that lead to recognition and identity and provide a degree of autonomy.

The traditional notion of an autonomy, which still persists, is explicit, being (using the same encyclopedia) 'in a political sense, limited self-government, short of independence ...'. What has changed is that with population increases these autonomies have become large unrepresented enclaves within states, strong enough, with modern means of protest, to be a threat to the majority and strong enough, also, to seek separation if a satisfactorily autonomous status is not forthcoming. 'Democracy' can no longer ignore the existence and implications of minorities within societies. Ethnocentrism is an extension of democracy, likely to destroy the traditional institutional concept of majority government.

The most important group excluded from a modern democratic legislature is, however, those who are excluded from political and economic systems by structural conditions which deprive them of political influence: the unemployed, youth with no role in society, single-parent families without means of support and others in poverty. There are also those on the margin who, while perhaps within the economic system, do not feel that they have a sufficient role in the system even to vote. 'Democracy' cannot be held to be representative of citizens in such circumstances.

All of this is understandable within the traditional power frame: minorities must be 'democratic' and accept their fate, just as historically females were expected to accept theirs and as teenagers still have to accept theirs. It points to the reality that alienated minorities can never be included within a system in the absence of deliberate constitutional provisions to bring this about.

Exclusions and the problem of corruption

These considerations raise a serious procedural criticism of democracy as widely conceptualized: that of institutionalised corruption. In the United Kingdom there is a frank acknowledgement by parliamentarians of what they term 'outside income'. This is pay from interest groups whom many members of the Parliament represent. This extra income is declared. The argument is that their salary of around £50,000, plus certain expenses, is not sufficient to attract to politics people of talent. There is hesitation is using the term 'corrupt'. But members claim that 'compared with any other parliament or democratic assembly in the world we are the least corrupt'.[1] The US Congress is far more influenced by organized pressure groups, but the term 'corrupt' is not used to describe the inducements involved. Yet a crime bill can be delayed and threatened by a gun lobby, and universal health coverage can be defeated by insurance company pressures.

These are serious criticisms of democracies as they have evolved. Nevertheless, it is these democracies that seek to impose conditions on other countries which, in their own circumstances, are pursuing other unsatisfactory systems.

To the extent that members of legislatures represent directly the interests of businesses or other pressure groups, they cannot freely represent their electorates. Looking to the future, and bearing in mind the identity needs of peoples that have to be met for political and social stability, there can be no confidence in modern democracies being the accepted model. In due course there will be, inevitably, a public reaction against their institutionalized practices.

Electoral processes

Members of democratic societies seem not to be able, given consensus beliefs, the media and education, to assess the obvious short-comings of their electoral systems. Party politics presents electorates with candidates selected by a very small proportion of the electorate, perhaps no more than 1 per cent or so in most cases. Voting for candidates is not only limited in the absence of compulsory voting, but is greatly influenced in favour of candidates who have large campaign funds and the support of interest groups. Those who experience structural conditions that lead to their violent and criminal behaviours are most unlikely to be represented.

There are, therefore, two core problems to be addressed. First, how to make legislatures more representative. Second, how to alter legislative decision-making processes so that, even though they may not be sufficiently representative, they become less adversarial and more problem-solving, and thereby more attuned to the needs of alienated minorities. To make legislatures less adversarial, more representative and geared to promote problem-solving conflict resolution throughout the society, the following issues deserve consideration.

Compulsory voting

Easy registration for voting may not be sufficient. Compulsory voting may be one essential provision that helps to ensure adequate representation of all segments of society. There are immediate reactions against compulsory voting as being in itself undemocratic because of the compulsion. But such compulsions are part of every society: social security registration, school attendance and others. There can be no rational reason for arguing that compulsory involvement in the representative process is a denial of freedom. It would, however, change permanently the composition of legislatures, as it is the alienated who have tended to regard voting as irrelevant to their condition.

In many countries in which legislatures represent only the more privileged, this would be difficult to bring about. But if attention were drawn to the fact that it exists in some countries, such as Australia, and that it does help to bring stability without threatening the system, it could find public support.

Proportional representation

'First past the post' in counting votes tends to exclude a large proportion of voters from any effective representation, even when second and other preference votes are included. Proportional representation is one means of giving effective representation to minority opinions.

Proportional representation has a major effect on parliamentary processes, making them less adversarial. If there are several small parties it becomes necessary for some of them to work together to form a government. Indeed, the more parties there are, and the more independents, the more co-operation and discussion becomes necessary.

Youth suffrage

Within a behavioural frame, for a legislature to be representative there must be, not only adult suffrage, but an adequate representation also of youth. Modern societies are facing a major problem with alienated youth. They have to be brought into society by whatever means are appropriate: education, jobs, representation and responsibilities. They have, as yet, few accepted means of having their case heard. Denied this, they have had to invent their own means of expression. The right to vote from fifteen or sixteen years, and preparation at school to exercise this right, would have many positive consequences in the behaviours of young people.

71

This, once again, directs attention to the need for community decision-making: the right to vote at community levels on issues such as school administrations, recreations and social conditions generally would bring young people back into the system.

Limited tenure

Tenure is an important consideration. There are advantages and disadvantages in all systems, but it does seem to be dysfunctional for representative roles to be held as careers or professions. Experience perhaps counts, but entrenched roles and continuing contacts with organized interests reduce the quality of electoral representation and increase opportunities for corruption. Limited tenure would make members of legislatures more representative and more responsive, and less influenced by interest groups.

Funding of candidates

The fact that less than 50 per cent of people vote in some countries is evidence that many people feel that they are not represented by the candidates selected by the usual party system. A growing number of independents in some countries is also evidence of this. Means need to be found by which to limit party expenditure on elections and to provide assistance for independent candidates to put them in an equally competitive position.

Decision-making processes

The way in which decisions are made within legislatures is, in practice, probably more important in dealing with social problems than are electoral processes. In an adversarial setting, minority viewpoints carry little weight. The structure of government and opposition ensures debate rather than constructive analytical discussion. In recent years there has been in many democratic countries an increase in committee work in many legislatures, but even this does not wholly break down the confrontational nature of decision-making debate. In a problem-solving frame in which there can be free discussion, as in a seminar discussion, all points of view can find expression, frequently revealing aspects of problems that are automatically rejected in an adversarial setting. There are many parliamentary and congressional rules that could be introduced without constitutional change which would lead to far more analysis of problems to be solved.

The physical set-up that places government and opposition in a physical confrontation mode could readily be altered so that representatives sat according to a listing of electorates, regardless of party. This would eliminate the perception of confrontation, with significant psychological side-effects on personal relationships. Parties are clearly an inevitable development when candidates need mutual support; but once elected there is no justification for injecting into the decision-making process the confrontations that are part of the election process.

This physical confrontation which reinforces party divisions is largely a carry-over from the past when, indeed, there were major interest gaps between classes. Increasingly such class-based divisions are giving place to divisions based on different means of attaining common goals. Frequently parties have similar platforms. Having adopted stances on means, they cannot afford, in the traditional mode, to alter declared policies, despite new data or insights.

The tradition of confrontation is outmoded as the issues to be resolved are complex social-economic ones quite unlike the early we–they protest issues which led to the present adversarial parliamentary system. Furthermore, the present party stances, which prevent legislatures from examining in open discussion policy issues that relate to the present and future interests of their electorates, are now being rejected by constituents who are increasingly favouring non-party or independent candidates for office.

The Speaker or President of assemblies could have an important facilitation role in ensuring constructive and analytical discussion. Behind the scenes this sometimes happens in some systems. But an acceptance of a role that included prevention of argument *ad hominem* and encouraging the application of normal analytical problem-solving processes, even a role that included seeking clarity on terms and asking relevant questions, could alter dramatically the party-dominated legislative process. Once again, this is likely to occur only when there is an understanding of, and a consensus in support of, problem-solving processes as an alternative to power political processes. Such processes have been learned and adopted by some local government and municipal councils in which party politics plays a less important role.

Logically, problem-solving decision-making would be promoted in the parliamentary system by the election of cabinets by the legislature as a body. In wartime multi-party cabinets have been, in some countries, the rule rather than the exception. Dealing with contemporary problems of long-term unemployment, alienation and violence requires no less co-operation between different political approaches.

Standing review processes

These are merely examples of the kind of changes that might be considered in order to bring decision-making more in touch with behavioural requirements, leading, thereby, to decision-making that sought to resolve problems by less confrontational means. For simplicity the focus has been on traditional Western two-party systems, but the same principles apply to multi-party and even single party systems. The aim in all cases is to evolve means of decision-making that are analytical and that serve longer-term interests as well as those of immediate concern. They are processes that represent viewpoints as expressed by the electorate, but they are processes which go further than this. They have the opportunity to take into account insights that emerge out of an informed analysis which might not yet be a part of public knowledge.

These examples, however, point to the need for continuous review processes built into legislatures, with a mandate to explore beyond existing and conventional procedures. Like all such review processes, they would require facilitation by some professionals not directly involved in party political politics.

While there is amongst political representatives an awareness of these confrontational problems in decision-making, there is little interest in dealing with them for fear of losing some power advantages. In March 1993 the then leader of the Opposition in the Australian Parliament made public 'Parliamentary Reform: Our Charter for the Future'. That opposition is now the government. It will be interesting to see whether reform is regarded as important to a party once in government.

Legislatures as an example

Reform probably depends on the mood of the electorate. It could, if given the chance, respond to platforms that were process-oriented rather than policy-oriented.

We concluded the chapter on leadership with the observation that it was only changes in many other social and political institutions that could deal with problems of leadership. This is not necessarily so with legislatures. They have the freedom to be innovative, to alter their processes and to be analytical about their own problems. Their members, obviously, have a vested interest in many of the norms that need changing, for example tenure, and even the public theatre of political confrontation. But it is they who are subject to a growing public disquiet about adversarial decision-making assemblies. It is their processes that can set the stage for changes in other social and legal systems that are adversarial and not directed to satisfying human needs.

Similar changes are required in decision-making processes in the home, in schools and at the workplace. An example set at the level of legislative decision-making could stimulate discussions and change at these levels also. Historically there are close ties between the confrontational nature of legislatures and we–they relations of the workplace. Workplace relationships are undergoing radical changes under pressures of global competition. Management versus labour and unions in their struggle for increased wages must now, in their common interests, give place to collaborative practices. This must also alter party political relationships in so far as parties reflect the past competing interests of management and labour.

Tribal and ethnic conflicts

Legislatures are a relevant consideration within relatively democratic societies. A large number of countries, perhaps a majority, are not in this category. At the time of writing there is tribal slaughter in the former Yugoslavia, Russia, Yemen, Rwanda and, on a smaller scale, in many other countries, such as Sri Lanka. These are largely a direct result of past aggressions and colonial practices.

Representative assemblies and legislatures are not possible in these cases. They will not be possible until there have been major adjustments in boundaries and steps taken to provide some degree of security, recognition and identity to the communities concerned. This will not happen while the preservation of the sovereign state remains the prime goal of states, for it justifies leaderships in their ethnic cleansing and other actions taken to preserve former colonial boundaries. Peacekeeping by a United Nations force merely perpetuates the conflict, as has been the case in Cyprus. South Africa has become a multiracial society, largely as a result of exceptional leadership, but it remains to be seen whether minorities will experience a sense of participation in the new system. It may transpire that separate autonomies within some nominal federal structure would have been a more behaviourally realistic system.

It is important in any holistic analysis of conflict to place the particular situation in the wider context of human history, as distinct from human evolution. Anthropological studies show that there have always been tribal clashes, frequently controlled by long-established conventions that limited damage and, indeed, contributed to functional relationships. What civilizations are now experiencing are understandable responses to conditions that have been imposed on peoples already suffering scarcities and environmental damage.

If there are possible solutions to these forms of conflict and violence they will have to include processes that bring to the surface the sources of conflicts, rather than placing blame on the parties now involved in the conflict. If this were to happen then the parties directly involved could be led to consider viable options. Third party interventions that merely seek to provide peacekeeping forces offer no prospect of success in solving the basic problems.

If separate autonomies were introduced into multi-tribal, multi-ethnic countries, a consideration of legislatures would be relevant. In contemporary conditions it is a consideration rejected by rival tribal leaders. There is still the major problem of undoing the colonial past. It can be tackled only by facilitated problem-solving processes. Perhaps this is the role of a major non-governmental organization supported and financed by former colonial powers.

Community government

These considerations take us back to observations made in discussing the structural frame in which an analysis of institutions needs to be made. Far more bottom-up decision-making is required, not only because of limits imposed on central decision-makers by the global economic system, but also because of problems of democracy and problems in decision-making itself.

The role of central authorities, by definition somewhat removed from the daily life of the peoples they are supposed to serve, is to establish a structure in which those closer to action can operate. In a federal system central authorities have separate states, which, in turn, have local governments to administer policies, which, in turn, have local councils to deal with day-to-day services. It is the role of the federal authority and states to promote agreed standards so that all authorities provide required minimum services at required standards. It is for the federal and state authorities to provide the necessary finance, by taxes and other means that ensure an equitable sharing of costs. It is essentially a co-ordinating role. Once a federal or state authority tries to take responsibility for defining and dealing with problems at the grassroots level, finance and administrative priorities push aside behavioural realities. Policies adopted do not prevent or resolve social problems.

The community emphasis, bottom-up decision-making, raises important questions, especially in the emerging global economy. Legislatures need constantly to be redefining their roles, reassessing their relevance, and exploring means of addressing community problems that are now threatening societies as a whole. Initiatives that would promote community organizations would probably receive popular support in the present conditions of insecurity being experienced by most people.

Note

1   R. Stevenson, *New York Times* (24 August 1994).

9

Academe and public servants

Academe and the public service can be examined together as there is a close connection in their activities, with frequent movement from one to the other.

Academe

In academe specializations prevail. Each of the separate social science disciplines still operates within the traditional power or compliance frame. The non-compliant human element, the source of social problems, is conveniently excluded from theory and its applications. 'Economic man' performs like a machine in predictable ways, as does the politically socialized person. It so happens that the policy deductions of this machine frame suit power elites and those who do not experience structural violence in any significant way. It is others whose human aspirations are frustrated by structural conditions, and it is assumed that they can be taken care of within the social and legal compliance frame.

Having brushed this human dimension aside, and with each discipline having its own construct, there exists no common base on which diverse specializations could come together and make reliable recommendations in respect of social problems. Social workers have one set of goals, eductionalists others, while economists pursue their investment and financial priorities without taking into account the social consequences and costs of deprivations due to poverty and unemployment which their deduced policies can create. Hence the 20 per cent alienation problem.

Bearing in mind public reactions to contemporary public policies in developed countries which seek economies by reducing educational budgets at all levels, it is a reasonable generalization to observe that there is no longer public respect for academe, except that part which deals with non-behavioural subjects, such as chemistry, physics and mathematics and new technologies such as communications and computers. Academe is a casualty of political trends towards reduced government expenditures because it has not played a significant role in dealing with the complex behavioural problems societies now face.

Public and civil servants

Public servants – like members of the family – have the potential of rendering their institutions either more or less adversarial in their practices. Like the family their institutions alter in structure over time in response to changing conditions. Like members of a family and of academe, public servants have their separate specializations and goals which make impossible any common base for policies.

Again, as is the case with members of the family, the adjustments made over time are rarely towards more collaborative behaviours. Like those in the family and in academe, public servants tend to be defensive in their responses to change. They feel threatened by those with opposing priorities and goals. Treasury economists have one approach, administrators in a labour or education department have others. They are in competition for funds, status and security.

On the positive side, the public or civil service, being for the most part a permanent establishment, provides continuity in administration despite changes in government. Consequently, to a limited degree, it mitigates adversarial party political stances. Could changes in public service structures and processes make its members less self-defensive and adversarial, and also make a significant contribution to a movement towards problem-solving at the political level?

The need for professionalism

All organizations have both policy-making members and those who implement decisions. In business there are controlling boards and managers. In government there are the formal political decision-makers, and administrators or public servants. The boundaries between policy-making and policy implementation are never clearly drawn because those defined as administrators have discretion in applying policies, and also an advisory role which is at times virtually decision-making.

Changes of government do not necessarily lead to changes in senior positions. Moreover, while public servants may have their personal political affiliations, they have an obligation to adapt to governing ideologies and policies, and also a career interest in doing so. The separation of the roles is, however, difficult when many senior public servant appointments are political appointments.

In the traditional Westminster system, political appointments are largely confined to senior positions. The appointees are, furthermore, frequently drawn from those already within the public service. There are now, however, in parliamentary governments, strong tendencies towards the American system, in which hundreds of presidential appointments are made, first to reward supporters, and second to ensure policy support. In the American system political appointments accentuate party political differences in public administrations. Now, prime ministers and ministers, like presidents and cabinet secretaries, no longer rely on permanent public servants for advice, but rather appoint their own advisers who become an *ad hoc* public service located in their offices.

Whichever the system, the clear need is for the highest possible level of professionalism. Such professionalism includes, but extends beyond, scholarship. It implies abilities to apply knowledge and, therefore, includes a high degree of administrative and co-ordinating abilities. There needs, however, to be a continuity of scholarship in the sense that practitioners should be constantly aware of research developments and should participate in research discussions on subjects relevant to their professional field.

There are serious problems, however, with such professionalism in addition to specialization problems to which reference has been made. Professionals generally are at least as removed from the realities of average social living conditions as the politicians they serve. They, like the scholars with whom they have worked, usually have had little experience or understanding of the endemic alienation suffered by the unemployed, minorities and any underclass there might be.

Furthermore, both professionalism and scholarship tend to be tainted with ideologies. It is for this reason that tensions are sometimes high within university departments and government departments, and between them. Economics as a discipline takes different twists that are more ideological than scientific: there are philosophies of intervention by government and those which suggest that the market should control, affecting policy views on employment, education, health and related policy areas, including a balance between present electoral interests and the needs of future generations.

Because academe and the public service are characterized by the pursuit of knowledge within discrete and separate disciplines, there is always a need for analytical discussion, the questioning of assumptions and re-definitions of goals. Neither academe nor the public service has institutionalized means of achieving this. Breaking up knowledge into separate specializations, and breaking up administration into separate policy areas, results in those concerned pursuing their interest areas with little input from other perspectives.

Democracies and legitimized dictatorships

Violence and crime often stem from poverty and unemployment, and these may be the product of all manner of financial and economic policies including interest rates, balance of payments, tariff policies and others. They also relate to social security, health, education, transport, housing and other issues.

Traditionally the co-ordination of public policies has been left very largely to ministerial or presidential cabinets at the political level. It is at this level that different departmental perspectives come together. But if there were to be a focus on a major goal such as reducing structural sources of conflict, rather than on immediate problems such as the containment of violence and crime, far greater co-ordination would be required at the investigative, analytical and advisory levels of public administration. This would require an altered professionalism and different administrative structures. It would require more cross-fertilization between disciplines at the investigation stages.

This is as difficult to achieve in administrations as in academe, for the same reasons. Experience is that professionals rarely change their interest areas, their approaches, their basic assumptions and theories, their ideologies, despite the availability of new empirical evidence and insights. Once a frame is internalized and applied to a career, questioning the validity of any part of that frame is felt as a career, or even a personal, threat.

One way out of these difficulties would be to give elected governments the right to remove public servants and to replace them with persons who share their ideologies and major priorities. This is, indeed, what is beginning to happen, as already suggested. A second means, again already happening, is to privatize public services and to allow the market mechanism to determine systems and policies, and by structural conditions leave no option but compliance. Maybe this is the way to go, bearing in mind the complexities of decision-making in the welfare-state capitalist system. It is, however, a political and an intellectual escapism which leaves untouched the increasing problems of conflict, violence and crime.

An example

Before proceeding further with an analysis of public administrations and the need for constant reassessments of relevance and changes in the light of altering circumstances, it is useful to take a specific example of a government department and to examine it from a non-adversarial, problem-solving perspective.

The one selected for examination is a foreign office. This may be removed from general experience, but it is one appropriate in any discussion about moving institutions from their traditional adversarial past towards a more problem-solving orientation in the emerging global setting. A foreign office is an example of an institution with fundamental structural problems which have been brought about over time through lack of questioning of relevance and of traditional assumptions, accompanied by a lack of appropriate professionalism. As in the case with leaderships and legislatures, there is resistance to changes which would threaten a tradition, and in this case, also, a way of life.

There has been little change in structures and attitudes over the centuries despite the break up of colonial empires with the increase of nation-states from 50 to nearly 200, and despite an evolving global system which is replacing the past system of 'sovereign' nation-states each with its separate and independent status. In addition there have been major changes in communications and travel technologies. There is no longer any need for 'sailing ship diplomacy', necessary in the past to promote interests in foreign countries in the absence of opportunities for direct communication. The changes in communications which have taken place in the last fifty years would have been beyond the comprehension of those who initiated diplomatic relations. It is now far cheaper and far more efficient to fly the relevant person from the relevant government department to foreign countries to negotiate with relevant officials there than it is to maintain diplomatic staffs. Fifty or so visits a year can be made from London to Paris for a week at a time for less than it costs to pay and maintain a diplomatic representative. Twenty-five or so such visits could be made from London to Tokyo. Going a step further, most negotiations can now be accomplished by direct personal communication between relevant people.

But there is an even more fundamental change, for which adjustments will be required. In the global system as it is evolving, foreign relations can no longer be separated from internal national relations. In the global society, every department of government has an interest in communication with others in other countries, whether it be health, education, the environment, drug-peddling or issues of justice. Direct communication with relevant people is as important as it is when officials in different states of a federation are dealing with matters of inter-state and national interest. Not merely is it as important, but technically it is no different. Officials and politicians in different states of a nation can readily discuss issues without previously knowing each other. They can do the same globally.

Within the national foreign office the structure remains as it was when the task was to deal with separate sovereign states. There are 'desk officers' who are specialists in the affairs of particular states and regions. These officials are well informed on current political and micro details – much of which can be obtained from the press. Trade and other officials, similarly, have special regions of interest. But in a traditional foreign office it would be difficult to find a 'desk officer' whose role it would be to analyse the nature of ethnic problems, especially those that cut through the boundaries of 'sovereign states'. Nor would terrorism as a response to structural conditions be a subject of professional interest. It is unlikely that there would be officials who would be aware of more recent thinking about the limitations of deterrence strategies. These broader and far more important information areas are outside the separate state and regional specialization frame.

Traditionally, the most important diplomatic relations, reflected in staff size and status of heads of missions, have been with the most friendly nations. This was because diplomacy was largely the cultivation of allies in an international system based on peace by power-balances and defence strategies. The most important diplomatic missions included, and still include, many military officers. Recent trends have been towards establishing stronger missions, especially where there are trading opportunities. If missions were to remain, and there were to be a shift away from an emphasis on defence strategies and trade, and towards conflict avoidance strategies, the strongest missions would be established where there were relationship problems to be resolved. There would not be military and trading representatives, which in any event should not have a diplomatic status, but those skilled in analytical discussion and getting to the roots of problems.

Not only is the traditional form of diplomatic relations out of date in technological terms. It is also unnecessarily adversarial because of its traditional structure and defence orientation. Current relations between the United States and its allies, and China, a country becoming more powerful in the traditional sense, are confrontational over trade, human rights, defence measures and Chinese claims to territories. There is little acknowledgement, perhaps little understanding, of the tremendous task involved in transforming such a huge country and population from a quasi-colonial status to one which seeks to improve living standards in a more equitable way. Its unique population controls, obviously necessary, have come under human rights criticisms, without any constructive alternatives being offered. This all reflects the adversarial nature of the now irrelevant power politics system.

There is now a global society constantly threatened by the spread of capabilities of mass destruction. These capabilities can be employed by threatened leaderships and other interest groups. A shift is required from the traditional power politics orientation in world affairs to a problem-solving conflict resolution mode. For this shift to take place there need to be fundamental changes in diplomatic administrative structures as well as in policies. In so far as there has been change, there has been some shift from strategic goals towards trading benefits. Indeed, policies in foreign countries which in the past would have stimulated protest, such as brutal repression of dissidents, are now quietly pushed aside where there are important trading interests to pursue.

These observations emphasize the need for a holistic approach to decision-making. In a foreign office the specialized 'desk officer' is not in a position to comprehend holistic approaches, especially their behavioural content. Still less are local representatives able to place the policies of the country to which they are accredited in a wider global perspective. For example, suppression of secession movements to preserve sovereignty is widely supported by locally accredited representatives, as for example in Indonesia and Sri Lanka. At the specialized level thinking is based on selected data and political arguments that apply to particular situations.

Policies require some co-ordination process, the bringing together of different points of view, and different descriptions of situations from different perspectives, within an explanatory frame that applies to all. This would require a group of officials and political decision-makers to be analytical in an appropriate frame. Such a group could probably perform their policy-making role without micro data from their diplomats and 'desk officers', making irrelevant many thousands of officials. In fact, this is what happens in war or in an emergency when decisions must be made at short notice. Such decision-making now takes place in ministerial offices because of the impossibility of useful consultation with a foreign office as presently structured. But it is taking place in an arbitrary way, responding to pressures and party political considerations, leaving governments without foreign policies which are consistent and predictable.

A foreign office is a useful case study because it demonstrates clearly the need for a conceptual frame from which can be deduced policies. The traditional power politics frame is clearly irrelevant to present circumstances. Presently there are no clear principles of policy in East or West on which there can be reliable prediction of policy. Immediate national interests, including short-term trade and corporate interests, internal needs to bolster leadership images and party political expediencies determine policies which lead to unpredictable consequences, frequently tense political relationships and military demonstrations.

The alternative frame outlined in Part One introduces the behavioural content necessary for the analysis of conflictual situations at all social levels, including foreign relationships. Within such a frame of analysis the answer to key questions which determine policies can be deduced. Is it appropriate to support foreign governments in their suppression of secession movements by military means? Is the sovereign state concept any longer the appropriate guide to policy? Should there be military support to an existing sovereign state as was the case in Vietnam? When there are ethnic conflicts are there processes which could be offered to resolve them? Is a free market a necessary requirement for peaceful relationships between countries? To what extent should other policy considerations be subject to the pursuit of trade opportunities? If answers to general questions of this order were deduced from the frame of analysis, policies in the particular case would emerge without reference to most of the material which is the concern of the 'desk officer'. Deductions from the general frame would guide policy, and predictions of policies could readily be made by other governments. Ministerial directives would not be required in most particular instances.

Public service generally

Similarly in departments dealing with conflictual goals or priorities, such as in industry, or in health and education in which funding is a major source of conflict, a public service which could help parties to be analytical and place their problems in the wider context of the whole of public policies could give less adversarial options to those at the political level.

In theory at least the public service has a major contribution to make in pushing political systems towards a problem-solving orientation. Whether the immediate problem is unemployment, crime or a security threat, the need is for a deep analysis of the total situation, and a holistic approach that ties the sources of different problems together. A public service can do this, however, only if its members are selected for the purpose and have the initial appropriate training and an adequate conceptual frame in which to make recommendations. They must also maintain contacts that enable them to keep in touch with emerging thinking.

Having failed to do this, public services in many developed countries have now lost the respect and support of the public they are supposed to serve. The perception the public has of them is that they enjoy their security of tenure and official perks, and their way of life generally, without playing any significant role in dealing with social problems. The alienated 20 per cent and members of the lower middle classes have no sense that they are being served by them. Members of the upper middle class prefer to have private health and education and other services rather than to have to pay for services for others. Thus governments score political points by privatization, by contracting out and by directly decreasing the number of public servants.

Both academe and the public service have a crucial part to play in tackling social problems, and in particular making public institutions less adversarial and more problem-solving in their activities. However, it is only their own members who can bring about the necessary changes in their structures and approaches. The future of societies probably depends upon them doing this.

10

The workplace

The workplace and the alienated

We have argued that the crisis in civilizations, the symptoms of which are conflict, violence and crime at all social and political levels, is largely due to structural conditions that deny personal identity to a significant proportion of populations. The origins of these structural conditions and their compliance nature are generally known. They emerged as societies evolved from face-to-face tribal communities to larger aggregations of peoples. These were necessarily organized on a hierarchical basis: even in early husbandry there were those who had ownership and social control and others from whom they demanded compliance.

Slavery was an early form of such social organization. Feudalism, under which land was made available in return for rent and services, was another. Gradually currencies and the wage system emerged, making possible industrialization and what has come to be termed capitalism. All these systems rested on control by those who had acquired economic and, therefore, administrative power. Communism was an attempt to share ownership and control, but it experienced unanticipated problems of management and incentive. All had, therefore, the potential of structural violence, for, in the terms of Lord Lloyd, 'the notion of authority is that some person is entitled to require the obedience of others regardless of whether those others are prepared to find the particular order or rule enjoined upon them as acceptable or desirable or not'.[1]

In economically developed countries, ownership has in recent years taken different market forms. The industrial struggle has become far less between owners and others and far more one between managers and workers, that is, between an upper and a lower middle class, those with high salaries, assets and investments, and those, perhaps renting or with mortgages on homes and facilities, who are dependent upon negotiated wages.

Now a global system is emerging. Forms of slavery still exist, including child exploitation, alongside wealth in most developing economies. In many cases military dictatorships persist as a means of containing the consequent structural violence. Industrially developed economies, previously isolationist and protectionist, are now making use of these exploitation opportunities elsewhere. The use of cheap labour in undeveloped countries has weakened the bargaining power of labour in developed countries. By eliminating many unskilled jobs it has also accentuated the 20 per cent alienation problem with far-reaching social consequences. Increased stress at the workplace, increased financial insecurities, unemployment, increased family and community violence, the use of drugs, are all merely symptoms of trends in this age-old failure to work out how societies can be productive without relying on ownership-control or management-control systems and the structural violence which is their consequence.

The workplace and adversarial relationships

It is probably the we–they relationship as a persistent feature of the workplace that initially established adversarial relationships throughout societies, including legislatures. The workplace has been and remains the dominant institution in societies. Relationships there inevitably carry through to all other segments of society, from the family to political levels. Now, in these altering market circumstances, adversarial relationships in the workplace are proving increasingly costly to society. Rarely are there incentives which would lead to more efficient processes or increased output. Where more participation by workers in decision-making has been introduced in some corporations there has been increased productivity. But more frequently industries seek to control costs in the emerging global system by introducing 'enterprise agreements', thus seeking to bypass wages negotiated by trade unions and to introduce individual bargaining.

The contemporary workplace problem

Changed relationships at the workplace are due largely to the consequences of technology and communications that have made large corporations, in some cases global corporations, the basis of many industrial structures. As populations increase and resources become scarcer, and as competition increases due to the use of cheap labour in developing countries, the corporate system will increasingly influence political and social conditions nationally and globally.

This corporate influence has positive and negative consequences. Large corporations are capable of and have interests in looking much further into the future than self-employed persons and small enterprises. They can afford to be innovative in dealing with employees, but they have little interest in environmental protection, especially when their industry relates to mining and products or processes which pollute. Within this global corporate system, national government is more restricted in its decision-making freedom. It is less free to impose trade restrictions, to maintain wage levels, or to divert resources towards education, health and welfare services. Nevertheless, specific government interventions are required to ensure that corporate programmes do not create social conditions that would ultimately damage the quality of life and the stability of societies. Governments are currently struggling to determine their mandates and to resolve problems of intervention.

In this chapter, however, the prime concern is with the contemporary and emerging workplace situation. Management and management studies have, in recent years, given some attention to improving relationships between top management, and white- and blue-collar workers. Extraneous activities to establish a corporate spirit are sometimes pursued, even climbing rocks and painting hostels in official time, just to encourage people to work together! Progress has been made in dealing with negotiable *disputes*. But little has been done to close the gap between management and routine workers and the treatment of the latter as machines without any personal or social identity.[2] Initiatives and decision-making on the shop floor are rarely part of management, and family and social responsibilities receive little consideration when determining working conditions. Consequently, in developed countries workplace *conflicts* emerge where those who are engaged in routine tasks experience a deep-rooted personal frustration or sense of deprivation resulting from an absence of any participatory role or recognition as individuals, and the sense of identity that recognition gives.

There is also a perception of injustice in rewards for labour as compared with management. The transfer of responsibilities and authority from ownership to management has not removed the sense of exploitation. On the contrary, while unions might be persuaded to bear in mind the need for competitive results in the evolving global system, management, frequently paid a million or more dollars, at least twenty times more than blue-collar workers, give themselves increased salaries and benefits.

The need for government intervention is clear, despite global competition. The precise types of intervention by authorities which are required are still to be determined. Probably it must rest finally on international agreements which governments can enforce. International Labor Office conventions have already played a small role. Far more intervention at this inter-government level is required in the new corporate global system if more serious consideration of a human dimension in the management of industry is to be given nationally.

The need for a frame

Communism, as attempted in the Soviet Union, sought to make the production of goods and services a shared social benefit, thereby seeking to eliminate the source of these workplace adversarial relationships. At the workplace the system succeeded reasonably well in so far as relationships between management and workers were concerned, but at the expense of efficiency, there being few work incentives. At the higher level of state authority the system failed. The separation of the workplace environment and quality of social life from political management suggests that the failure of communism in the USSR was a failure to overcome the power-elite management system it sought to replace. The Communist Party took the place of a privileged owner class. In the frenzy to catch up with the West and in the absence of adequate feedback, there were catastrophic planning mistakes and neglects, especially in the area of the environment. In short, the means employed to establish and to consolidate a non-adversarial society created even less acceptable we–they, adversarial relationships at the political level, and, in due course, at the industrial level also, leading to self-destruction.

Currently many hold the complacent view that this Soviet failure validates private enterprise systems as they exist. This ignores, however, the reality that systemic problems of unemployment and alienation, together with workplace frustrations and tensions, remain a serious problem in capitalism at all of its stages. Indeed, in a competitive global economy in which those individuals and nations which are 'rich' get still richer and the 'poor' much poorer, these workplace problems will continue to trigger demands for fundamental changes in employer–employee relationships, and also in relationships between participatory members of societies and their alienated underclasses.

It is relevant to observe once again that there is always a need for a behavioural frame in which to discuss a problem. In the absence of a comprehensive behavioural view of their relationships, negotiations between employers and employees in a system of private competitive enterprise become merely aggressive–defensive bargaining situations. If employers impose conditions on employees which disregard human elements, there are necessarily all manner of unexpected consequences. If employee organizations are sufficiently powerful to influence outcomes, then there may be serious market consequences. Some collaborative process involving management, workers and national and global government seems essential.

The tragedy of the Cold War was that there was no frame in which to discuss and to be analytical. The options were communism or capitalism as they existed. There could be no admission of serious problems. The problems each system encountered were brushed aside as being merely the imperfections that had to be tolerated. There is now a return to the 1930s need to find an alternative or modified economic-political-social system. The corporate state seems once again to be the expediency option, brought about, not by any thought system and deliberate decision-making, but by industrial technologies and the international availability of cheap labour and of communications.

In both types of societies, free enterprise and planned, there are some in-herent human influences operating which have not as yet been precisely de-fined. In Soviet communism such needs may have been partly satisfied at the workplace, but not at a political level. In the private enterprise system they are certainly not yet satisfied at the workplace and less and less so at the political level.

A major leadership problem is also emerging within the workplace. While personal recognition in society may well be a human need, it does not follow that a drive for personal recognition at the expense of others is also a human need. Anti-social behaviours by entrepreneurs and managers are probably the outcome of behaviours required by traditional practice, rather than of any personal aggression. Performing a management role does not necessarily give satisfaction if there are obviously related adverse social consequences. In-deed, personal recognition is based on valued relationships and these are readily destroyed by activities which damage social cohesion. Structural vio-lence is not necessarily confined to those over whom authority is exercised. Those in control can also be victims of the system.

There is a basic dilemma between satisfying personal identity and recogni-tion needs through opportunities within the private enterprise system, on the one hand, and loss of quality of life and of valued social relationships, on the other. Experience shows that there are those who are system-driven in a com-petitive situation and who will seek their psychological and material satisfactions even at the expense of society as a whole. This may lead to temporary successes, but it also frequently leads to corruption as is reported daily. Private enterprise plays to such persons. To prevent this by authorita-tive constraints would deny opportunities for such personal development while failing to provide alternatives. The challenge common to all management systems is to find processes by which individual human needs can be fulfilled and social harmony secured while achieving production goals.

In a free enterprise society quality of life and the social good generally take second place to initiatives for individual leadership roles and for material achievement. In undeveloped conditions especially, the power and leadership roles dominate. As societies develop economically, a middle class and those with aspirations to belong to such a class generate an 'I'm all right, Jack' philosophy which ensures that those who are underprivileged remain that way. It is not clear that this selfishness within a free enterprise system is a preferred option. Within the power management frame there appears to be no other.

Some economists have sought to justify policies that promote this trend. Economic 'rationalists' have argued that special incentives for potential inves-tors promote further growth. Inequalities in treatment are, therefore, an as-set. Reduced income tax on higher incomes, accompanied by regressive taxes on goods and services, are given a theoretical justification. An interim means of raising revenue is privatization of government enterprises – health, education, communications, transport and even security. Ultimately such policies must be self-defeating: as inequalities increase, consumption demands correspondingly decrease. In any event, the deprivations resulting from such policies are the foundation of a violent society.

We are led back to the question whether the free enterprise system has the answers societies seek and, if not, what are the options? Can there be a form of society that makes possible widespread satisfaction of human needs? It would seem that it must be an interventionist system, but one in which the principles and goals of intervention have yet to be determined.

Innovations in workplace relationships

Centuries after the formal breakdown in Western countries of serfdom systems, after the introduction of parliamentary democracies and in conditions of global competition, the continuing organized division between employees and employers has become an absurdity. It is self-perpetuating largely because it is institutionalized and alternative options are still untested. Outdated political-ideological sentiments and supportive institutions serve to reinforce these divisions.

In some countries attempts have been made, as already observed, to do away with agreements with unions and to substitute enterprise bargaining, that is agreements within particular companies, sometimes protected by governmentally enforced minimum standards. But these are resisted by existing unions for fear of their consequences, including the elimination of unions in the absence of any assured government interventions to protect workers, even though many workers within particular industries might favour direct negotiations.

The problem would be reduced if there were conditions of full employment, giving the individual employee opportunities, not merely to bargain from a position of greater strength, but to find alternative employment. But governments and their economic advisers still fear full employment conditions. Juggling levels of employment is the preferred means of control of inflation, balance of payments and other economic and financial conditions. There were attempts to introduce full employment as an international obligation back in the 1940s at International Labor Organization conferences and at the drafting of the United Nations Charter. But strong resistance from developed countries resulted in no more than weak declarations of intent.

There is a growing recognition of the need for worker participation and a sense of personal identity. In one company in the United States there are committees which are comprised of elected workers who review applicants for jobs and organize some production programmes. These give a sense of participation and have led to increased productivity, and to saving the company administrative costs.[3] There are experiments in adjusting to employee needs for private time, such as a four-day week.[4] These are no more than early signs that a major problem is being recognized.

In some industrial societies there are some attempts to bridge the social gap between management and workers. In Japan, for instance, there has been traditionally a far lower degree of adversarial we–they relationships than in other industrial countries. There has been greater security of tenure. Global competition is challenging the tradition. In Germany and in some other European countries there are work councils which provide a 'second channel' for communication between management and the workforce. In many cases these are mandated councils as, for example, under the German Workers Constitution Act. The United States and the United Kingdom are exceptions in this emerging pattern of dual channels for worker representation, despite strong empirical evidence of the increased productivity that could result.[5]

Given a behavioural frame, it is possible to deduce basic principles to be observed in evolving a productive workplace relationship. They are no different from those already discussed at the political level. Management needs to operate in a facilitating role, bringing together the viewpoints and interests of all. Policy-making needs to be collaborative and problem-solving, thus involving workers as well as management and directors. To promote full commitment in workplace responsibilities, there need to be built-in processes to enhance the quality of life, to lessen work stress through fear of unemployment, to provide for child-care and to ensure further educational opportunities.

There will be no long-term solution of the we–they problem in industry unless the society in which industry operates is a more egalitarian one. Income differences for management and worker roles would need to be greatly reduced by government intervention, such as taxation policies, making the two roles less separate in rewards, in social perceptions and in practice. At the outset it was made clear that any searching analysis of problems of leadership, policy-making and other institutions must be made by the parties concerned. This requires constant reassessment of role and relevance. This must be done, however, within a relevant frame for discussion and with the assistance of a facilitator whose role would be to ensure that the frame was observed. In this case the parties are not just management, unions and government. Workers and citizens need to be involved as people. It is interesting to speculate what outcome would result from intensive analysis by participants that was, first, problem-solving rather than bargaining, second, conducted within a behavioural frame and, third, conducted with an awareness of the consequences to society of the absence of some resolution of this problem.

The literature

There have been few references to other writings in this analysis. This is despite the existence of a most extensive literature on conflict management. The reason is that the frame of this analysis differs fundamentally from the traditional we–they power frame which still persists in discussions of conflict management. There are many examples in the recent literature of approaches, especially in management studies, that acknowledge a human dimension. The term 'human' is sometimes in the title of books. But on closer examination, they all remain within the traditional we–they frame. They merely advocate taking some psychological elements into account when attempts are made to gain co-operation in increasing production in the short term. They do not address the long-term problem of alienation, and consequently fail also in their immediate aims. In *Workplace 2000: The Revolution Shaping American Business*, Joseph Boyett and Henry Conn make a thorough review of developments, including those referred to above. An understanding of the 20 per cent problem of alienation and exclusion from society is, however, still lacking.[6]

Furthermore, even the more forward-looking analyses in the management area focus on how to get the best out of management personnel and other white- and blue-collar workers. Little attention is given to we–they relations between managers and other workers. This may be partly because routine workers in large corporations are now frequently living in underdeveloped countries. There they are treated in a way not far removed from the slave tradition. Indeed, their rewards may be less than slave labour in that slaves were maintained, whereas in many cases routine workers employed by corporations in underdeveloped countries are rewarded with less than the costs of existence, frequently lacking accommodation and necessary health-care. If they choose to complain or can no longer work, there are others to take their places.[7] Routine workers within developed countries, though better paid, are similarly not regarded as persons with human attributes.

Even the recent literature on leadership in industry is grounded in traditional approaches. The notion of strong leadership, providing guidance as though leaders know all the answers, still characterizes the literature. This becomes clear when leadership is defined in terms of its duties. These duties include definition of goals, values, motivations, management, unity in management, acting as a symbol and a representative.[8]

Costs and change

But there are exceptions. There are the writers, such as John Mathews, who focus far more on change and means of change rather than on management to preserve traditional we–they relationships.[9] A new area of study is implied, which is the goals and means of change.

With the recognition of human elements in the workplace, that is, the need for recognition and identity and work satisfaction before productivity can improve, there have been strong trends towards greater participation in decision-making. Mathews argues that political pressures will ultimately ensure radical changes in relationships at the workplace:

> But political pressure, no matter how strong or seemingly over-powering, will be dissipated if it is not channelled in an effective manner. Unions and employers on their own, even in the best of all possible partnerships, cannot change the industrial system. The role of governments and social movements, professional groupings and other 'associations', will also be critical. A framework of goals is needed to tie these disparate interests into a coherent force, and orient them towards a common goal. I suggest that this goal can best be described as 'economic' or 'associative' democracy, conceived as an extension of the labour movement's historic role in achieving political democracy.[10]

Notes

1 D. Lloyd, *The Idea of Law* (Harmondsworth, Pelican Original, 1964).

2 K. Johnson, 'Corporate Conscience', *New York Times* (21 July 1994).

3 J. Holusha, *New York Times* (2 August 1994).

4 *Wall Street Journal* (3 August 1994).

5 J. Rogers and W. Streeck, 'Workplace Representation Overseas', in R. Freeman, ed., *Working under Different Rules* (New York, Russell Sage Foundation, 1994).

6 J. Boyett and H. Conn, *Workplace 2000: The Revolution Reshaping American Business* (New York, Nal-Dutton, Plume Books, 1992).

7 R. Rothstein, 'The Global Hiring Hall', *The American Prospect* (Spring 1994).

8 J. Gardiner, *On Leadership* (New York, Free Press, 1990).

9 J. Mathews, *Tools of Change* (Sydney, Pluto Press, 1989).

10 Ibid., p. 184.

11

The legal system

The overburdened legal system

A legal system, like legislatures and the workplace, is part of our inherited tradition. It shares the confrontational, adversarial frame. Just as there are government and opposition, and management and workers, so there are in the legal frame prosecution and defence in criminal trials, or in the case of civil disputes, plaintiff and defendant. Professional ethics and tactics historically decree that there be limited contact with the 'other side' lest discussion and more understanding weakens the case of either in this adversarial setting.

There are two major influences that are at last altering these norms. First, the legal system is no longer an effective means of social control. Because of increased structural violence and its social consequences, the burden on courts has become too great. The costs of the legal process deny many access to the system. Alternative processes are being explored. These include pragmatic, administratively expedient 'Alternative Dispute Resolution' processes. It is not clear that this substitute negotiating system is an advance where there are behavioural issues involved, though sometimes it does bring the parties together.

Second, those within the legal system, especially some judges who deal constantly with cases involving alienated persons, are becoming aware of the importance of the human factor. It is they who are beginning to realize that legal processes, including punishments, are not a just or a socially effective means of dealing with crime. They point, for example, to domestic abuse associated with drugs and alcohol, and when they have before them juvenile criminals they sometimes question whether the appropriate persons are in the dock. They are not necessarily pointing to parents, for there are other circumstances, such as unemployment, for which systems are responsible.[1] In short, those dealing with crime are becoming more interested in sources.

The empirical evidence is confirming the doubts of those who work directly within the legal system. There is now strong evidence that deviants placed under strict detention become less, not more desirable citizens. In

Australia, 'Around 50% of people in gaol commit another crime once freed.'[2]
Yet the detentions continue at an enormous cost per head which could be
used both to help to eliminate the conditions which led to the deviance in the
first place and, in the meantime, to assist the individuals concerned in over-
coming the structural problems they have encountered.

This is not an option entertained by most decision-makers, typically removed from such realities. In 1994, during discussions of a Crime Bill in the
United States, one senator made the comment that the proposed legislation
was unacceptable because, in addition to spending funds on more gaols and
police, there was to be expenditure also on crime prevention. He commented
that this could lead to appointing more extra social workers than additional
police. No one thought to respond with the observation that this might be
more effective and that upper-middle-class societies, in their own interests,
should be prepared to afford both until the problem is resolved.

Conflict resolution

While judges and some advocates are worried by the limitations of the criminal system, conflict resolution processes are difficult to integrate into legal
thinking because conflict resolution challenges its basis. The origins of conflict resolution thinking lie in theories of behaviour which suggest that in
certain circumstances there can be no deterrent controls, leading to behaviours which are outside the possibilities of personal choice. From these theories it is possible to predict that, in the absence of institutions that provide for
the satisfaction of basic human needs, there can be no social stability such as
is required to make law and order possible. This is challenging to those within
the legal system, but realities are forcing some rethinking.

Three different approaches to social control are therefore emerging: first,
law; second, the pragmatic or expedient Alternative Dispute Resolution; and
third, conflict resolution. The pragmatic approach emerged out of law and
the over-burdening of the legal system. Like law it is the servant of existing
institutions. The pragmatic must be treated as a temporary or transitional
phenomenon. It lacks any theoretical foundation or justification and has
emerged only by default. Conflict resolution has emerged out of certain theories of human behaviour and of empirical evidence of human responses to
unacceptable societal conditions.

The longer-term future will, by necessity, be a combination of law and
order processes, in which preservation of social structures is the goal, and of
analytical problem-solving conflict resolution processes, in which human
components are the basis. The bringing together of these two seemingly opposing approaches will be via progressive changes designed to accommodate
human needs both in institutions and in the legal processes which preserve
them.

As already indicated, analytical problem-solving conflict resolution does not have its origins in the tradition of social controls, but in evidence that such controls are not always effective and, also, in explanatory theories of behaviour. Holistic theories of behaviour have emerged because it is not possible to throw light on social problems by examining them from particular disciplinary perspectives. Conflict resolution, however, throws light on the short-comings of many legal processes.

Law and conflict resolution as complementary

What is predicted here as inevitable in due course is a redefinition of the role of law, incorporating problem-solving conflict resolution. This would enhance a public awareness of the nature of such problem-solving and complement trends towards prevention of damage done in family, school and social relationships by altering community services, counselling and education – in fact, social conditions generally.

The link between legal processes and conflict resolution lies in the appropriate training of those in the legal profession. This should, in practice, be acceptable to them. Attorneys have a duty to represent a client in what appears to be a win–lose situation. Even winning may not necessarily solve the problem, as, for example, in cases of custody disputes. Furthermore, in an adversarial situation in which decisions are based on available empirical evidence there is the possibility of serious misinterpretations of evidence in the absence of a deep analysis of conditions and motivations. There are cases in which persons are found guilty of crimes largely because of a reliance on limited empirical evidence. A child may commit a serious offence, but the conditions which triggered the behaviour could place responsibility elsewhere. The 'soft on crime' approach is reasonably resisted by many, but the 'soft on structural and social change' approach is no less reasonably advocated. If punishment is found not to be a deterrent, the hard approach has to be reconsidered, at least to the extent of applying the hard approach to the parties really responsible.

With such complexities to be taken into account, not just in the interests of justice, but in the interests also of more effective procedures, attorneys need to work together in the interests of their clients and society. They could agree that in some cases a preliminary step would be for clients to consult, perhaps with them present, a professional in the problem-solving area.

Lawyers, obviously, have an important role to play in breaking down the adversarial nature of legal processes and introducing into them a capability to cater to a human element. A start would be to include these issues in training courses.

This does not mean that legal processes as they now exist would become wholly irrelevant. There are cases in which traditional legal processes are appropriate, and others which require the input of conflict resolution.

A generalization would be that *disputes* which are confined to interpretations of documents, and disputes over material interests in respect of which there are consensus property norms, fall within a traditional legal framework. *Conflicts* which involve non-negotiable human needs must be subject to conflict-resolution processes. These would include many cases of crime and violence.

These distinctions, however, are often difficult to make in specific cases. It is not until they are being treated that their nature is revealed. This points to the need for a close working relationship between the two approaches, rather than different professions acting separately.

Law and order as a social problem

Altered training of lawyers and changed processes allowing for the facilitated resolution of conflicts would have positive results. But the ultimate solution is outside the scope of the legal profession. Provention requires altered social conditions, for example the elimination of unemployment and other sources of alienation.

In Australia in 1994 the government considered a report on long-term unemployment which clearly argued that such unemployment, while being an important economic problem, was also a major social problem. What had been regarded for decades as an economic problem was belatedly recognized as being of far wider concern. So it is with anti-social behaviours and with personal conflicts. It is not chiefly their control or settlement that is important, but their prevention by appropriate social policies. Unemployment had done its personal and social damage before it was defined as a social problem. Apparently gaols must get fuller, police forces more widespread, neighbourhood watches institutionalized and expensive defence precautions taken, before crime and personal conflict will be recognized as the product of social problems to be resolved rather than merely to be punished and contained.

Once again, the reluctance to acknowledge realities is due very largely to the fact that it is those who do not suffer who have the power to determine the nature of institutions and their processes. Economists do not have a direct link with the human aspects of unemployment. They, therefore, treat employment as a mechanism for financial and economic control. Lawyers have no role in assessing the consequences of economic and social deprivation and must be content to treat crime and conflict as an inevitable condition of social relationships. It is only when security becomes a problem for all that thought is given to the nature of the problem. Unfortunately, those who could contribute to prevention of conflict, violence and crime are far removed from its social consequences. If more information was available about all the sources of conflict, violence and crime, both from the perspective of the victim and of the perpetrator, public and media attention might focus on those, including the legal community, who have responsibilities to act.

Notes

1   See a letter from Judge Eugene M. Hyman, Municipal Court, Santa Clara County, California, *New York Times* (25 July 1994).
2   Corrective Services Department, NSW, 1994.

12

The international system

The notion of structural violence can be applied to relationships between nations at different stages of development and with different economic and military capabilities. At the international level exploitation and repression have been severe in their consequences. Over the years occupations of territories and colonialism have broken up tribal communities by the imposition of boundaries, and 'natives' have been relegated to a slave status without possibilities of development. This has been, indeed, structural violence.

Now structural violence is taking another international form as corporations take advantage of cheap labour in developing economies. One consequence of this is unemployment in developed economies. The contemporary global industrial and communication systems have eroded the decision-making freedom of even the most powerful of nations. In the past, central authorities had constitutional powers that enabled them, not merely to exercise influence throughout the nation, but also to control foreign influences to a significant degree. The central authority could impose trade restrictions and control financial transactions. Such powers provided central authorities with means by which to support industrialization, promote employment and generally determine social and economic policies as though the nation-state were a separate unit within the wider international system. But in the global system the central authority within a nation-state has to be far more aware of international competition and is no longer free to pursue its own national policies. The need to reduce costs of production is putting pressure on wages and levels of employment.

Peoples in developed economies are beginning to experience declines in living standards. Economic cycles will, in future, be fluctuations in economic activity, not in a rising curve of productivity, but in a declining one. This is making it even more difficult for governments to tax those with higher incomes to maintain welfare, education and health services. The gap between the 'haves' and the 'have-nots' is increasing.

The progressive shifts from the 'billiard ball' or nation-state international system, that is, separate units in contact with each other at their boundaries, to the 'cobweb' interactive or functional system which includes links between internal parts of these otherwise separate units, and then to the global system in which boundaries are not a barrier to transactions, are dramatic paradigm shifts that have taken place over a time-frame of no more than half a century.[1] The adjustments that are required in response to such shifts are no less dramatic. While the nation-state remains a legal or constitutional entity, it has limited administrative powers by which to control its destiny. The global system is making the traditional centralized nation-state an anachronism. The limitations on centralized power to determine standards to be observed in the workplace, and to make available social services, leads to their privatization. With quality and higher education only available to those who can afford it, there must be increasing inequalities in opportunities and incomes, with far-reaching social consequences over the longer term.

The limitation of the decision-making powers of nation-states, including those of the great powers, has not as yet been brought to public attention. National governments are still being held responsible by their electorates for decreasing living standards, unemployment and violence. It is little wonder that books such as *The Costs of Living: How Market Freedom Erodes the Best Things in Life*[2] are reflecting disquiet, but without being able to home in on the sources of the problem, for these have not yet been articulated.

One major example of limited decision-making freedom at the national level is in relation to major corporations. While the national activities of international corporations are, from a legal perspective, wholly under the control of national legislative decisions, in practice control over them is limited. If government decisions are not in their interests, international corporations have the option of production elsewhere: factories can be closed, creating sudden and widespread unemployment, and production can be shifted to another country. National and local authorities have to carry the costs of supporting displaced workers and of consequent social problems.

In practice this means that national branches of international corporations have a tremendous bargaining power, sufficient to influence decisions about local conditions in their favour. Wages, conditions of work, tax laws and means of financing health coverage and minimum welfare can no longer be determined by national considerations alone to the extent that it was assumed to be possible within the earlier nation-state system.

The trends in this direction will continue. The global economy includes increasing limitations on national abilities to impose trade restrictions and protections. Locally based industries must conform more and more with global working conditions if they are to remain competitive. Developed countries can anticipate working conditions comparable to those of developing countries. In 1994 President Clinton of the United States recognized that this prospect was likely to become a mainstream public issue. He suggested that labour and social standards should be the focus of the next round of trade negotiations once trade restrictions had been tackled.[3] He did not seem to realize that it was US pressures to eliminate trade restrictions that was a major problem for developing countries.

Functional international agreements

There are many trends within the global system which reflect the endeavours of nations to protect their independence. One way of dealing with the emerging situation is to bring nation-states into functional agreements that would exercise some of the controls internationally that they previously sought to exercise as independent nations. For many decades there have been various international functional agreements, governmental and non-governmental, that govern health, communications, air transport and the many matters that are of inter-state concern. Non-governmental organizations, such as the International Labor Organization, those concerned with transport, the environment and other areas of concern, continue to extend agreements. Perhaps in the future there could also be global minimum wages, workers' compensation for injury, pension systems and other such safety nets which developed countries have been able to introduce, but which they now find they must limit for reasons of competition.

Regional authorities

A trend in the defence of national independence within the emerging global system has been for nations in the same region to try to work together and to protect themselves against global and greater power pressures. The European Council is one such attempt. But this has run into difficulties because of the existence of quite different industrial structures, as, for example, in the United Kingdom and Germany. Similar developments are beginning to take place in the Asian and other regions. To the extent that they are successful, regional agreements play into the hands of business enterprises within these regions as they can then cross boundaries without restrictions.

Such a development has within it the seeds of its own destruction. By merging into a common decision-making body, the members deny themselves their own autonomy and identity. Regional organizations create an even greater central authority, which adds to problems at the community level rather than helping to resolve them. Ethnicity and related social problems are likely to escalate. Regionalism is a defensive response in conditions in which there needs to be more, and not less, attention to human behavioural requirements. For example, preservation of agriculture and particular local industries and ways of life could be important from a cultural point of view to all citizens in a particular country. Farmers in France have organized protests to direct attention to their plight. But membership of a regional economic organization continues to threaten local agricultural and industrial structures, despite cultural and related implications.

The market mechanism

Another state response to corporate and related global systems is for government authorities to opt out of their regulatory and social responsibilities and to let the market take over. Deregulation and privatization have become widespread in developed countries. Expenditures that would require increased personal income and corporate taxes are cut to enhance competitiveness: health insurance and health care, education, even the running of prisons, have become increasingly the responsibility of private enterprise in some countries. Indirect regressive taxes, like sales taxes, take the place of income tax for fear of decreasing market investment incentives – justified on grounds of 'economic rationalism' – adding further to the income and social gap between 'haves' and 'have-nots'. Trade restrictions remain unacceptable, not only to global corporations, but to many economists. Yet the social consequences of global competition, including sometimes slave conditions and child exploitation, have to be faced.[4] Governments cannot permanently evade this problem.

In adjusting to global conditions, and especially competitive conditions, states are adjusting to the existence of unacceptable conditions in competing countries. Child labour in one country necessarily leads to unemployment or decreased wages in others. Such conditions lead to defensive and frequently aggressive measures, such as sanctions. Conflicts, including wars, are primarily a spill-over of pressing domestic situations.[5] Unless state authorities can respond to the consequences of the emerging global economy, the result must be increased international conflict, despite increased mutual dependencies.

International corporations and national problems

Many, if not most, major global corporations are based in developed countries. They still depend upon them for their markets. For this reason some pressure on them can be imposed by developed nations working together to observe some welfare conditions internationally.

This is not necessarily an impossible option given the nature of corporations. International corporations are not like the businesses that were the foundation of *laissez-faire* capitalism, that is many small units, making possible competitive conditions. Altered production techniques and changed international relations have led to corporations that survive only by operating as global oligopolies. Large corporations are ongoing institutions with a status not unlike those of nation-states, and certainly with more influence than many nation-states.

Just as states have had to adjust to global circumstances over which they have little control, so global corporations must adjust to realities. There is every probability that major international corporations will, in their own interests, move towards self-regulation, especially in relation to the environment, but also in relation to working conditions. Some major corporations are already joining together to consider economic and, therefore, ecological sustainability.[6] But major developments towards such a longer-term perspective have yet to occur.

In practice such a trend would require national governments to work with corporations to mandate conditions that all must observe, for it would need only a few not to observe such agreements for competitive conditions to undermine their ultimate objectives.

Further developments of the global corporate system will take place once a major population like China becomes part of the international system. Reports from China point to the way in which, despite political controls, private enterprise, legal and illegal, is expanding rapidly in response to information from developed countries now available by internet, radio and television.[7] Similar developments in the former Soviet Union, the Middle East and Africa will change the global system more in the decade or so ahead even than has been the case in the last decade or so.

The role of the state

While corporations may be capable of looking after their employees, and even of taking a longer-term view of environmental and related problems, one consequence of their activities is to make a substantial proportion of a population, especially in developed economies, irrelevant to the economic system. These are the unskilled or routine workers who have been replaced by foreign subsidiaries. Their fate is not a corporate concern.

Yet it is the alienated long-term unemployed, youth unemployed, minority unemployed, who have no role or identity in their societies, who are a source of many social problems. Global trends will result in a loss of identity and the alienation of a critical proportion of populations of developed economies becoming a continuing feature of the life of nations in the future. No longer will there be any shared sense of effective participation in decision-making in dealing with these problems even in the most democratic of countries.

Still less can the global corporate economy deal with the pressing problems of the post-colonial countries and their ethnicity, war-lord, resource depletion, slave-labour conditions and associated problems. These will continue to be an aid drain on those countries that can afford to make some limited contribution in a crisis situation.

Strategic issues

In terms of defence and strategic issues, national governments are caught between two quite different worlds. There is the global economy which is inevitably causing costly problems in developed countries, and there is the political world of separate states requiring increasingly costly interventions by these same developed countries. Decision-makers, especially those in more militarily powerful countries, are at a loss when challenged to take a lead in some situation of terrorism or calamity in another nation. They are expected by their own peoples and by the international society to act as in the past. But, with modern weapons, they now face far higher costs of intervention, and also far higher costs in lives, and perhaps failure and its consequences. On the other hand, international institutions do not have the capabilities to deal with any such situation. Many of their members are involved and are on the defensive, and there is neither the military might required nor the problem-solving experience.

It is the United Nations which is supposed to have the capacity to deal with situations of conflict. However, the United Nations, an international organization comprised of independent nation-states, many of which have their own internal problems of minorities seeking separate autonomies, is becoming irrelevant in its present form. Founded at a time in which power balances and power politics were the consensus means of international law and order, it has not been able, for reasons which are examined below, to adjust to the failures of deterrent strategies and to move towards provention and to problem-solving in any particular situation.

A short history of the United Nations gives some insights into the present dilemma. The United Nations Charter was signed at San Francisco in June 1945, coming into force in October of the same year. At the time of its signing the United Nations Charter was widely regarded as a creative and forward-looking document. The original Dumbarton Oaks draft was the result of intensive work by the Allied Powers. The San Francisco conference gave the opportunity for a detailed examination by other participants, resulting in many amendments. The Assembly and the Economic and Social Council were both given an increased role, reflecting the approaches and interests of the smaller powers.

One important clause in the original draft was the veto power which the United States insisted upon as a condition of membership. A proposed amendment to eliminate the veto power failed at the Charter Conference to gain the required two-thirds majority only by a few votes. At the time the United States and the then Soviet Union, allies in the struggle against Germany, were still working together in a supportive way. This made the veto seem to many of no great significance.

The Charter reflected the thinking of its time. It was wholly within the traditional and prevailing power politics frame. It is accurate to assert that there was no delegate at San Francisco who had any concept of problem-solving based on a facilitated analysis by the parties to a conflict. The organization to be formed was to be devoted wholly to maintaining peace by peace-keeping and peace-making operations as determined by the Security Council. Indeed the members, being nation-states, would seek to ensure the preservation of sovereignties, including existing boundaries of states, against any secession attempts. Ethnic conflicts within member countries were not in the minds of delegates at the Charter Conference and no thought was given to how to deal with them. Indeed, they were in the category of those matters which were wholly a matter of domestic jurisdiction. In the 1960s the two communities in Cyprus, Greeks and Turks, were separated by United Nations peace-keeping forces. To do otherwise would have been to imply an agreed separation and to set a precedent for secession within a nation-state. Twenty-five years later those forces are still there.

It was believed that deterrence strategies pursued by the United Nations would deter aggression and control potential conflicts. It never occurred to members to consider any alternative to the power frame, such was the thinking of the time. Furthermore, it was assumed that the permanent members of the Security Council, the United States and the Soviet Union in particular, would remain in harmony and ensure that the Security Council would be in a position to enforce its decisions.

Historically the United Nations will be seen as a post-war form of colonialism. It initially comprised fifty nations. As post-war independence movements developed, commencing with Nehru's India and extending throughout Asia and then Africa, numbers were increased to three times that many. It still does not include 'unrepresented peoples', that is all those disgruntled minorities within nation-states which will at some future date, if they do not already, demand to be recognized as separate autonomies.

The end of the Cold War

It was not many years before relationships among the permanent members of the Security Council changed and they returned to their previous pattern of confrontation. Technological developments brought with them increased mutual tensions and threats, requiring increased defences, while the power frame which prevailed ensured a lack of communication, false perceptions and every apparent reason for escalating arms production and deployment. The United Nations, having no facilitating processes by which to handle such confrontations, was irrelevant to this 'Cold War'. It was also irrelevant to the increasing number of conflicts, ethnic and other, which consequently emerged within and between other member states.

The 'Cold War' was, of course, a term used to describe the continuing tense relations between the former Soviet Union and the Western democracies led by the United States. When in the early 1990s one of the parties seemed to disintegrate, it was reasonable to argue that this particular Cold War had ended.

However, this limited conception of the Cold War is of relevance only to those whose concern is with the particular and the immediate, rather than with the future prospects of conflict and its avoidance. In the broader context of global relationships this particular Cold War did not end. It has been transformed into many wars, cold and hot. Not only are there wars amongst autonomies within the former Soviet Union, some of which have a nuclear capacity; but the so-called ending of the Cold War has allowed the surfacing of widespread leadership battles, ideological and ethnic conflicts and territorial disputes, both within the former Soviet Union and elsewhere. The former Cold War powers are no longer motivated or able to intervene in the conflicts taking place in and between smaller countries. These seemingly separate wars become linked as involved parties which have shared ideologies and belief-systems seek mutual support. In this respect the Cold War has merely changed some of its features. The threat of major global thermonuclear conflict has given place to many actual conflicts which together result in high levels of death and destruction. It has also given place to rivalries, previously suppressed for strategic reasons, between one of the Cold War actors, the United States, and other rising major economic powers such as Japan and China.

If the perceived new world order leads to unchallenged demands by the remaining superpower, the United States, on others to observe so-called human rights, particular trading policies and forms of government, the Cold War will spread beyond Russia and its associated autonomies to China, Japan and other countries, large and small.

This would be merely the repetition of history. In the Great Depression period of the 1930s Western colonial powers, especially Great Britain, began to pursue domestic policies that protected their textile industries. This deprived Japan, an island economy dependent on sources of raw materials and markets, of access to British markets and those of its Asian and African colonies. Thus, as a response to conditions imposed by the domestic interests of the then more powerful Britain, another cold war emerged, soon to become a very hot war, finally involving atomic weapons.

In a similar way we could examine sources of conflict in relation to North Korea and Vietnam, and in Central and Latin America. In each case domestic politics in the United States, and attempts by more powerful nations to impose their will on the less powerful, were essential sources of conflict.

Vietnam provides an instructive case study. There were clear domestic reasons for US interest in Vietnam, not least of which were the US domestic politics of anti-communism. In Australia there was a debate as to whether the internal Vietnamese conflict was the pursuit of communism, or a struggle for independent nationalism. The debate in Australia and events that led up to the Vietnam war have been well described and documented by John Murphy, in his *Harvest of Fear: A History of Australia's Vietnam War*.[8] This book describes by implication how domestic and foreign politics mix, and how governments are prepared to be involved in wars for ideological and domestic political purposes. Records now show that those in Australia who adopted the 'domino theory' of communist aggression did so largely for domestic political reasons, and also to keep on side with the United States and ensure its continuing involvement in the region.[9]

In short, examining particular conflicts and their features suggests that it is superficial to refer to the end of the Cold War as though it were a historical watershed. The leadership and domestic political conditions that contributed to it remain. Furthermore, they are global, affecting countries small as well as large.

Listed below are some of the causes of cold wars that persist. These are an important part of the international structure in which nations-states must respond.

1. Political leadership ambitions. In recent years there have been so many examples of leadership ambitions leading to warfare that documentation seems unnecessary. It is a general phenomenon, not confined to the United States and United Kingdom, despite glaring examples there. Political leaders seem to be prepared to sacrifice lives for personal political purposes. This is a major problem – perhaps the most important problem in contemporary conflictual relationships. The problem has been articulated by Paul Kennedy in his *Preparing for the Twenty-First Century*,[10] and by Jeffrey Carten in his *A Cold Peace: America, Japan, Germany, and the Struggle for Supremacy*.[11] Until there is a consensus that leadership should be a facilitating role, bringing different viewpoints together and encouraging an analytical rather than an adversarial approach, the fact that aggressive leaders gain popular support will continue to be a source of many conflicts.

2. Ignorance of behavioural inputs. Leaders and governments fail to cost accurately the political and military consequences of their policies – wars are started and lost by those starting them. The reason has to be ignorance of human responses and a belief that the threat and use of military power can reliably alter behaviours. The theory that deterrence deters still dominates academic and political thinking. Thinking has been so power-oriented that acknowledgement of human responses and the consequences of the use of force has been limited: failure has been credited simply to not enough force being employed.

3. Adversarial political institutions. The Western political system, characterized by adversarial institutions, promotes confrontational policies, leads to misperceptions and is a major source of conflict, as has already been argued in previous chapters.

4. Interest groups, especially the arms industry. This hardly needs spelling out. Societies seem to have come to terms with the realities of arms promotion, believing that nothing can be done about it. This is especially so in conditions in which interest groups can determine political decisions. It is significant that, despite the popular belief that the Cold War has ended, the arms trade continues to flourish. Smaller countries are a growing market.

5. The availability of weapons. Disputes, such as tribal boundary and ethnic disputes, which in the past did not reach high levels of violence, are now occurring between parties that are armed with modern weapons. In many cases these are made available by Western countries in which the arms industry exercises decisive influence on governments: party political and leadership interests and short-term industrial and financial expediency result in arms exports that overshadow longer-term national and global interests.

6. Trade and commerce deprivations. Great powers have gone through their own protectionist phases, but now demand that small states conform with their free-trade interests. Demands made on developing countries by developed countries have, for domestic reasons, to be resisted. This is becoming an important source of dispute and conflict, even between major powers such as the United States, China and Japan. For smaller and developing countries there are sound economic and cultural reasons for production diversity as there were in days past when countries like the United States and Australia relied on protection to become industrial.

7. Boundaries. The global society is still in the colonial phase so far as boundaries are concerned. The newly independent states have been reluctant to make changes to their sovereign possessions. For example, the Organization of African Unity from its first meeting resolved not to alter existing boundaries, even though they were established as a result of colonial invasions and frequently cut across tribal and racial territories. Consequently, there are many ethnicity and autonomy problems. There is a reluctance on the part of greater powers to allow them to be tackled for fear of a threat to the principle of sovereignty. A seminar at the US Institute of Peace included a discussion on 'Does any group of citizens have an inherent right to secede – even forcefully – from an internationally recognized state?'. Ambassador Max Kampelman argued that 'self-determination is a limited human right encompassing cultural independence ... But it does not include the right to change boundaries at will because that is destabilizing.'[12]

8. Unrepresented peoples. The United Nations is comprised of states that seek to defend their existing boundaries, despite demands within many of them for separate autonomies. There are many non-represented peoples, some of whom have formed their own organization. The real explosion has yet to come. The United Nations, seeking to preserve the sovereignty of its members, will be seen to be wholly irrelevant in this emerging global society.

9. UN interventions. The United Nations has not been able to tackle conflicts at source. There is a strong resistance to any analytical conflict resolution process, for this would necessarily raise questions of territorial sovereignty and ethnicity. The United Nations has rested on 'peace-keeping' by military means, leaving the core problems unresolved. Its interventions probably do more harm than good in the longer term. To the Secretariat and Members of the United Nations, intent on defending their sovereignties, 'problem-solving' means preservation of the *status quo* and peace-keeping by military means.

10. Intelligence organizations. Intelligence organizations maintain that they exist to save democracies from themselves. A government can be elected on one platform, but can then act in quite different ways without a mandate, perhaps in ways against the national interest. While it is not stated, intelligence organizations assume a political and philosophical knowledge greater than politicians and scholars. They are the institutions that can unseat governments and demolish persons whose policies they disagree with. They have representatives at diplomatic missions, thus forming an international network pursuing its own ideological goals, regardless of government policies. They are part of the power frame, in which contact with potential enemies is subversive. They have no conception of a problem-solving frame in which such contacts are the means by which to preserve security by proventing or resolving conflict.

11. Deceptions by governments. Related to all these causes are the deliberate deceptions that governments promote for their own domestic and leadership reasons. The domino theory was used to attract support for the Vietnam war and the extreme anti-communist policies of the United States. The post-war independence movements of Asia were described as evidence of communist aggression. Deceptions and manipulations of public opinion are not unusual, and they become a major source of escalated tensions and conflict as has been documented by Jonathan Kwitny and others.[13]

It is within this international structural frame that institutions within nation-states must now determine their policies, striking a balance between the requirements of global competition, and the use of traditional power strategies to secure advantages in addition to genuine security needs. With such complexities foreign policies can no longer be traditional power responses to changing circumstances and situations, and must be facilitated analytical problem-solving processes so as to arrive at an accurate assessment of relationships.

Notes

1   J. Burton, *World Society* (Cambridge, Cambridge University Press, 1972).
2   B. Schwartz, *The Cost of Living. How Market Freedom Erodes the Best Things in Life* (New York, Norton and Co., 1994).

3 R. Rothstein, 'The Global Hiring Hall', *The American Prospect* (Spring 1994).

4 Ibid.

5 J. Burton, *Global Conflict: The Domestic Sources of International Crisis* (Brighton, Wheatsheaf Books, 1984).

6 For example, 'Business for Social Responsibility' in Washington DC and 'World Business Academy' in California with branches in other countries.

7 O. Schell, *The New Yorker* (25 July 1994).

8 J. Murphy, *Harvest of Fear: A History of Australia's Vietnam War* (Sydney, Allen and Unwin, 1993).

9 P. Edwards with G. Pemberton, *Crisis and Commitments* (Sydney, Allen and Unwin, 1992).

10 P. Kennedy, *Preparing for the Twenty-First Century* (New York, Harper and Collins, 1993).

11 J. Carten, *A Cold Peace: America, Japan, Germany and the Struggle for Supremacy* (New York, Times Books, The Twentieth Century Fund, 1992).

12 USA Institute of Peace, *In Brief*, 42 (September 1992).

13 J. Kwitny, *Endless Enemies: The Making of an Unfriendly World* (New York, Congdon and Weed, 1984).

Part Three

Towards consensus change

In Part Three we turn to practice. What does it take to move from a system based on an elite compliance frame to one that is process-oriented and directed towards avoiding and resolving social problems?

Change is a major problem for all societies, and the problems of change are explored in Chapter 13. Deliberate change, as distinct from change due to gradual environmental, technological and social evolution, implies intervention by some authority. The argument that there needs to be deliberate intervention by authorities to promote harmonious relationships, and in particular to avoid serious violence such as occurs in ethnic clashes and 'world wars', raises the question whether there is an intellectual and political capability within societies to bring about the kind of consensus change that would resolve problems and prevent them occurring. This question is tackled in Chapter 14 in which it is asked if and when intervention is desirable.

Any intervention, however, must take a holistic approach, otherwise the attempt to deal with a particular problem will create others. This is dealt with in Chapter 15. The means of doing this is to focus on decision-making and in Chapter 16 it is argued that much more bottom-up decision-making is required if problems are to be dealt with at source. Finally it is relevant to examine how education and public awareness can lead to consensus agreements on these issues. This is done in Chapter 17. Conclusions are summarized in Chapter 18.

13

Problems of change

Societies are organized to preserve their institutions and social norms. Constitutions are one means. They are not designed to encourage change and adjustment to altering circumstances. This is reasonable and understandable. But there is a down side, especially in conditions in which uncontrollable change, such as population increases, resource depletions, alterations in relations between sexes, emerging ethnicity consequences of past colonialism and so forth, requires social adjustments.

Decision-making is the starting point

Our main theme has been how civilizations can adapt to changing conditions so as to satisfy the basic human needs of people in constantly altering circumstances. The answer must be, not in new systems, but in decision-making processes that constantly reassess the relevance and effectiveness of existing institutions and policies and, thereby, progressively alter each from that which exists to the agreed goals of its members.

In such ideal circumstances it would be reasonable to expect a high level of social conformity, despite some unacceptable conditions, pending imminent change. In such a situation members of a society could be expected to display a social conscience and tolerance pending change. When, however, there are accumulations of required changes, with little or no prospect of any being made, both direct protest and the indirect protest of apathy and anti-social behaviours can be expected.

The types of conflicts that are threatening contemporary societies are those in which no change is anticipated. An industrial dispute could lead to a strike, but if there were some prospect of serious negotiation and change such action could be avoided. Delays in negotiations have led to violence in Northern Ireland and Palestine. In South Africa there are black citizens who were thrown out of their agricultural holdings and who, under the new regime, seek to regain them. If there is some reasonable prospect of settlement they are likely to be patient. If not they are likely to take their own action. Alienated black youths in American cities perceive no prospect of change. They see no evidence that their plight is known to or being addressed by relevant authorities. Their anger is directed against society generally, and against their own peoples in the absence of any other outlet. Ethnic minorities in underdeveloped countries see no future for themselves except that which they create for themselves, by violence against others if necessary.

The ideal condition of tolerance and social conscience is not possible, therefore, when there are accumulations of required changes and an absence of clear programmes to alter conditions. It follows that, not only is continuing change required, but also clearly articulated prospects of change when there must be a time gap between the perception of the need for change and the implementation of change.

This calls for legislatures and administrations that are perceived to be aware of the nature of social problems and willing and able to come up with solutions. The party political system, and the adversarial industrial system, do not offer this prospect. The alienated 20 per cent, in particular, see no prospect of change in their favour.

Political conflict: social stability versus change

Behind the adversarial decision-making approach, which is a feature of modern societies (as distinct from early face-to-face communities), is a dilemma that has not received appropriate attention either at a decision-making or at a research level. On the one hand, relationships in all societies rest on a common acceptance of social norms or rules. These are different in different societies, resulting in different cultural norms; but the learned observance of a set of social norms is an essential requirement for members of any species, human or other, to exist as a group. Norms and rules, usually enacted into law in civilized societies, are by nature static, permanent and a symbol of stability. Constitutions help to ensure a continuing order and political-social stability. On the other hand, social norms and rules, if they are to be observed voluntarily and without coercive processes, must be adjusted continuously to meet altering individual and social needs in altering circumstances.

The requirements of stability thus create conditions of instability. This is particularly so when, over time, rules or norms are determined only by those within a society who have most power. The rules become their property and are used to preserve their roles and interests. In an adversarial political system a ruling elite reasonably resists change, brushing aside the possibility that change sought by those advocating it could lead to a more secure and less conflictual society.

There is, therefore, an evolutionary dilemma. Societies require orderly procedures in relationships between members. But alongside this form of stability and as part of it, constant adaptation to altering conditions is required if societies are to meet environmental and social demands made upon them, and if they are to avoid destructive problems occurring.

This dilemma becomes a focus of analysis within a human needs frame. If it were the case that deterrence deters, that law and order could be enforced, that members of families, societies, or nations, could be required to conform, the dilemma would not be a concern. If this is not the case, there is a serious problem to be resolved.

It is this dilemma, and what to do about it, that is the underlying issue in contemporary party politics. There is obviously something missing: some procedure by which to bring together two seemingly contradictory elements in the one social stability process. Both sides of politics have a wholly reasonable and understandable case: those who take the side of social stability, and those who focus on the sources of instability and the need for change. Obviously, fighting between the two sides can never resolve such a dilemma. Ultimately both sides seek the same thing, a stable and just society, but neither side credits the other with this goal.

As in any conflict situation, each side perceives the shared problem from one particular perspective. They are no longer divided only by class. Any congress or parliament in modern times has members on both sides who are wealthy as individuals. They are where they are not to represent capital or workers, but because they happen to perceive a shared problem from a particular perspective. Being on one side or the other forces them to take stands that wrongly identify them with the privileged or the underprivileged. To the extent that they represent or respond to special interests it is probably more because of direct inducements from organized pressure groups, and frequently representatives on both sides receive inducements from the same pressure groups.

In such circumstances it can be anticipated that neither side can come up with the answer to conflict, violence and crime related situations, for neither side sees the situation in its full context. There is a problem to be resolved. It can be resolved only by processes of analytical problem-solving that take into account all aspects, not by political party confrontations that focus on different aspects.

The change process

Even a totally democratic, wholly representative decision-making system could readily legislate in ways that proved destructive of societies in the longer term. Even the most thoughtful of interventions can fail to shift institutions and norms in the direction of harmonious and productive relationships. Theories, such as a human needs theory, are guides. But altering circumstances, values and ideas, many of which cannot be predicted, must be accommo-

dated. While alteration of systems and their institutions must be in an appropriate behavioural frame, there also needs to be an ongoing process of reassessment which involves all parties concerned, guided at the time of
decision-making by all available theoretical knowledge and by experience.
Contemporary legislative and decision-making processes are reactive to altering conditions, but are typically not participatory, analytical or problem-solving. While the goals of political parties have, in developed countries, moved
towards a centre point, the adversarial processes have changed little.

At a micro level, industrial structural change is a good example. Management studies show how necessary it is in the cause of efficiency to adjust to
changing social circumstances and, in particular, to cater to the personal
needs of workers. But in practice few managements do this. In altering social
conditions more women with children are entering the workplace. But parents are rarely provided with suitable facilities, resulting in absenteeism.

Such considerations reinforce the observations made in Part Two about
the nature of leaderships, legislatures, public servants and all decision-making and management institutions. Unless and until they can become problem-solving in their processes, no policy solutions will be found which will
cope with globalization and emerging environmental, population and resource
depletion conditions.

Changes in the global society

Elite control, which has been the dominant feature of societies, has been
regarded as having some positive social benefits in providing a degree of stability in constantly evolving conditions. This view has prevailed despite experience of accumulations of needs for change, which have led in due course to
revolutions and wars. In contemporary conditions not even these periods of
stability are possible. Environmental, social and economic conditions have
been altering fundamentally at an increasing rate. As Robert Reich has observed, production no longer falls into the three categories by which national
economies have been described in the past – agricultural, manufacturing and
service industries. The division of labour is now between 'routine production
services', that is, repetitive tasks requiring little skill that can be performed
anywhere; 'in-person services', which are also routine but must be performed
at specific locations; and 'symbolic-analytical services', that is, the planning,
professional and consultative services that are required for manufacture and
for research. People in developed economies seek employment in this third
category in their own and in other countries, relying on the people in underdeveloped countries to supply labour for routine jobs that do not have to be
located alongside symbolic-analytical services.[1] Despite these fundamental
changes, the affected institutions, especially the free market, are protected
and the 20 per cent problem is pushed aside.

The result is the emergence of third world type enclaves, an underclass, within developed economies. No amount of superficial juggling of revenues and expenditures can deal with social problems on this scale. The two systems, the market and welfare, now separate and in competition, need to be brought together so that there will not be continuing decreases in support services, such as education and health, leading to increased alienation and conflict.

This raises the politically sensitive issue of taxation through which the market finances welfare services. This, in turn, raises an issue which is, understandably, rarely discussed: the value societies attach to material development, measured by the Gross National Product, justifying the promotion of investments, and the value attached to Quality of Life, justifying more welfare services and, therefore, higher and more progressive taxation. No longer can it be asserted that increased GNP promotes increased QOL.

Continuing conflict and violence at all social levels are measures of continuing instability. Anticipating and planned interventions are now a necessity, despite complexities and a defeatist inclination to hand over to the marketplace. And unless these interventions are made consciously within a behavioural frame, unless they are problem-solving, taking into account the long-term needs, values and interests of all concerned, they will fail to bring stability. Quality of life must now be inserted into calculations.

Central legislatures are limited in their decision-making capabilities in respect of those social problems which lead to conflict, violence and crime. In tackling these complexities responsibility for decision-making needs more and more to rest on community administrations and communities themselves. It is at this level that social problems can be defined and the specific problems of the neglected and alienated 20 per cent taken into account. The role of a central authority is to co-ordinate local policies and provide the financial, economic and social conditions required to eliminate the conditions identified at the source level where crime and violence occur.

The irrelevance of 'Left' and 'Right'

Practical experience leads to the conclusion that private enterprise supplies incentives which are indispensable in the struggle to make efficient use of scarce resources. At the same time controls are essential if there are not to be widespread environmental depletion and social violence. Responses to this dilemma have traditionally been interest-based and ideological. But in the new set of circumstances there is no reasonable option but to take a more objective or analytical view and to determine interventions that are required over time to ensure a continuing response to change and an adaptation to economic, political and social systems and relationships. The traditional Left—Right dichotomy is, in modern circumstances, irrelevant. It still dominates party politics in most countries and binds participants into untenable positions. Adversarial politics must give way to collaborative problem-solving, and this requires analytical approaches free of competing ideologies.

Reich observes that 'symbolic analysts will become even wealthier; routine producers will grow poorer and fewer in number; and, with the enhanced mobility of world labor and the versatility of labor-saving machinery, "in-person servers" will become less economically secure'. But he adds a comment that points to the need for an analytical rather than an ideological approach: 'The peace of mind potentially offered by platoons of security guards, state-of-the-art alarm systems, and a multitude of prisons is limited.'[2] No longer is it sensible for employers and workers, producers and consumers, the governed and their governors, to confront each other on public issues: all share problems that must be resolved in their own interests. That interventions are required should not be an issue: the issue is what are the kinds of intervention that are needed.

The need for viable options

The most effective controls are probably those that are undertaken voluntarily, that is, those that promote future self-interests. Much must depend on the spelling out of a constructive future. If costs to the tax-payer or consumer were to be seen in the context of a more secure future, then there would be less resistance to controls by appropriate authorities. This is why analytical problem-solving decision-making seems to be the only viable option.

There is as yet no name for such an option. History is a history of power systems. From the family to communities, to nations and to the international society, power has been a determining consideration. Systems have been named and defined in terms that suggest where power lies. Feudalism, mercantilism, industrialism, capitalism, communism, fascism, majority-democratic government, all have had their own sources of coercion and control. Now societies have come to the end of this road. Analytical conflict resolution provides a new process, not a new system. It takes what is and provides means of change towards agreed social goals. It provides an input into all systems, regardless of type and at whatever stage of development they might be, which moves them in the direction of a harmonious society. Agreed system change becomes routine when institutions have built into them means of reassessment of relevance.

Notes

1   R. Reich, *The Work of Nations* (New York, Vintage Press, 1992).
2   Ibid.

14

Natural evolution versus intervention

Is intervention desirable?

Have members of societies and their political and intellectual leaders, working within the institutions that have evolved over time, the capacities to deal with the complex problems that civilizations face? These problems include population increases at an exponential rate, similarly increasing resource depletion and environmental pollution, ethnic conflicts, youth alienation, social violence, corruption and crime of many kinds which seem presently to be beyond authoritative control. If adequate intellectual and institutional capabilities for determining consensus goals and achieving assured outcomes do not exist, clearly substantial interventions by authorities should not be attempted. If nothing better than *ad hoc* band-aid solutions are politically or technically possible, it may be better to leave economic, social and political problems to be dealt with by those who influence the natural evolutionary process, that is those who have political, military and police power and power in the marketplace. Their interventions would be limited to enacting provisions that would provide the legal and social norms required to obtain consistency across this power system. It would then be left to private organizations and local communities to address their problems as best they can. Indeed, this is very much the contemporary position in many major developed countries, and the trends are persistent elsewhere.

The naturalist view

An evolutionary or naturalistic view, a non-interventionist view, cannot be dismissed lightly. Trying to save and indefinitely to maintain starving peoples in regional conditions that cannot support them, curbing resource exploitation at the expense of employment opportunities, seeking to curb violence between ethnic groups who compete for territory, providing for the health, education and welfare needs and aspirations of an underclass are, in the naturalist view, exercises which do not achieve the longer-term social goals of societies. They merely drain resources from those who are productive and on whom the future of civilizations will finally depend. In this naturalistic view, the contemporary problems of societies and civilizations are frequently the direct result of well-meaning but misdirected interventions that perpetuate problems. For the achievement of social goals there should be greater reliance on the humanitarian good sense that is an inherent part of functional human relationships.

Economics as a study includes macro- and micro-level theories of development that are consistent with this non-interventionist approach. *Laissez-faire* market control, the 'unseen hand' of Adam Smith, in theory eliminates incompetence and rewards efficiency. Policies based on such economic rationalism discourage regulations which govern employment conditions and the right of organized labour to enhance the bargaining position of workers. They seek to leave control of bargaining between employers and employees to the better judgement of employers and employees, both of whom must have in mind their shared long-term interests, such as the need for worker co-operation and incentive, and the need for profits. The naturalist view is that similar non-interventionist policies should apply to all situations and relationships at all social and national levels – severe droughts, disease control, ethnic conflicts and others – for these are the natural controls on population growth and resource depletion.

This philosophical outlook has become more widespread in recent decades, as is evident in trends towards policies of deregulation and, in many developed countries, reductions in the proportion of resources made available by governments for education, health services and social benefits. The private sector has tended to increase in these fields. What has emerged is a pragmatic social outlook that enables the materially and intellectually advantaged to pursue further their material interests. While there is no direct acknowledgement that the system has adverse consequences for others, there is a tacit acceptance of responsibility in limited obligations to meet the essential welfare needs of those who have been adversely affected by natural disasters and economic conditions over which they have no control.

Intellectual capabilities

Politically, when ethical, moral or social issues – however they might be described – are brought to academic or public attention, a practical consideration has to be faced. There may be a direct causal link between a freely developing society and adverse social conditions for a minority; but must this not always be the case? Is there the intellectual and administrative capability to avoid and to resolve the complex problems of societies?

There appears to be a growing consensus that authorities, and the political institutions through which they work, are in many cases incapable, not merely of organizing societies so that there is greater social justice and less frustration and alienation, but also of responding appropriately to environmental deterioration and to changing resource and population conditions. Authorities are held to be incapable, not necessarily because they lack ability, but because of the magnitude of the problems.

One 'post-modernist' approach to social problems seems to rest on the belief that emerging social problems are too complex for intervention strategies, and may be best left to social responses to events rather than be the subject of some theory-based interventions. The post-modernist doubts are justified by experience to date. If leaders and scholars, and people generally, do have problem-resolving capabilities that can be applied to social-political problems, certainly there has not been much evidence of it. Where there are situations involving scarcity and competition, skills have been applied to pursue the primitive goals of competitive acquisition – survival-of-the-fittest – that arise out of scarcities and out of the struggle for personal recognition. There is little historical evidence of abilities to resolve political and social problems either within or between nations.

Intellectual capabilities and interests

Population problems and the burden of an underclass and of poverty obviously have to be dealt with in ways that do not inhibit the abilities of those who can make the greatest contribution to economic development. No one would reasonably disagree with this proposition which is so central to economic rationalism and to opposition to a planned economy. But this is not the issue. The question that is troublesome is how such persons, groups or institutions can be given the necessary freedom and incentives to be creative and productive without creating conditions that, finally, will not only create a violent underclass, but also destroy the opportunities and life-style of valued achievers. This is especially troublesome in conditions in which, without controls, there are exponential population increases and unnecessary resource exploitations, and in which those who are a burden to achievers have the means by which to be destructive of the environment and of developed societies.

The argument that was put forward in Parts One and Two was that an adequate theoretical frame, one that includes a behavioural component, reduces complexities and makes problem-solving possible by providing a focus on the ultimate source of complex social problems. By so dealing with complexities, problems become more, not less, manageable.

One reason for what seems to be an intellectual incapability could be that thinking about social, political and economic issues has tended to reflect the immediate and relatively superficial interests of the educated and privileged in societies. The power frame of the free market can seem more attractive to achievers than a problem-solving one that anticipates the future and wider social requirements. As a result there have been failures to perceive accurately events and trends as they emerge.

Many examples of fundamental misperceptions can be given. A simple but important one that leads to wrong definitions of social problems and to dysfunctional policies is in relation to problems of 'recessions' and 'depressions'. They have been treated as temporary setbacks of only limited seriousness for those affected. Short-term unemployment relief has been a remedy. But these problems are probably no longer due to fluctuations in a permanently *upward* resource-exploitation curve, as was thought to be the case when populations were smaller and when exploitation capabilities were less effective. Now these fluctuations are probably within a *downward* curve, downward because of the extent of resource depletion and increased populations. These fluctuations are, consequently, more severe and prolonged, leading to long-term or permanent unemployment in the absence of appropriate policies. Typically, elite policy responses are to increase resource exploitation and investment still further, so as to offset unemployment and increasing poverty. It is likely that Keynes was right, that such a policy makes matters worse, and that what is required is a more egalitarian economy, directed more to quality of life than to stimulating investment. But this perception is rejected by the majority of educated people who benefit from existing institutions and policies.

One encouraging consequence of failure is that at least some institutions and structures come under scrutiny. For example, the party political system, once regarded as an essential feature of Western democracy, is now seen by electorates to be absurdly confrontational. It has become associated in the public mind more with personal interest and party bickering than with public-interest action. The democratic majority control system is also under scrutiny wherever there are ethnic and other minorities who feel alienated and insecure.

But being under scrutiny is not in itself a positive process. Doing something about a situation requires an accurate definition of the problems experienced, including accurate assessments of past causal trends and of their future influence. Environmental, resource and population trends are known to most people. Far less is known of the influences that have led to decreased quality of life, to increasing levels of deprivation and alienation and to widespread violence. While there is an adequate literature, authorities and societies seem not to be aware of, or do not wish to acknowledge, for example, the problems alienated youth have in seeking recognition and a role even in their gangs, and who welcome a term in gaol to show that they have undergone initiation and have won through to adulthood. There has been little official investigation into the complex problem of family violence that examines its major sources and does something about them.

If attempts are to be made to break away from an evolutionary 'cure', such as leaving all policies to the free market, then the intervention process must be supported by all possible intellectual capacities. A first step is to seek explanations of emerging problems and to arrive at a theory that points to the cause of problems, from which to deduce appropriate institutions and policies.

Self-defeating possibilities

Many interventions now seem to be essential. The world population now doubles within forty or so years. Unnecessary environmental pollution and resource depletion must further limit economic development and the quality of life. The costs of violence domestically and internationally are likely to increase exponentially in the absence of problem-solving measures. A non-interventionist approach could lead to some population control by disasters, but not sufficient to make a difference without intervention strategies to control population growth.

In short, civilizations are at a transition stage. It is this which has created a crisis situation. Human aspirations and needs seek fulfilment. They are proving to be stronger than authoritative controls and stronger than market influences. Adam Smith was describing only the political and social conditions in which he lived. But now a human power has to be taken into account that could undermine societies established within the free market system.

The interventionist approach

No general principles of intervention that would help to answer questions about the nature and the goals of the decision-making institutions of societies have emerged in political thinking. Where there are elected governments, political platforms are based on specific policies, not on principles of intervention. Typically countries alter party leaderships regularly. Change usually reflects dissatisfaction with government policies and performance rather than endorsement of the alternative policies. The reversion to some form of naturalism, reflecting failures in intervention policies, is a persistent tendency. Failures in both approaches, intervention and non-intervention, frequently lead to extremes in both.

The key questions, therefore, are what interventions are desirable, by whom and for what purposes? Whether or not the naturalist approach is more realistic and logical, and whether or not interventions can be successful, some interventions will continue and probably increase as social, environmental and resource problems increase. Some foreign aid programmes and domestic welfare programmes will be pursued, along with interventions designed to assist free enterprise in the global economy.

In practice a compromise between these two approaches takes many forms. In developed societies there is an understandable reluctance to provide more than symbolic assistance for those in other societies who for reasons of disease, climate, resources, ethnic competition for territory and control or other influences, are likely to be destroyed or to destroy themselves. There is also the same reluctance to help those in the same society who are deemed to have failed to acquire their own resources for shelter, health and education. Their failure is rarely attributed to system faults.

The degree of compromise between the naturalist or libertarian and the interventionist approaches, and the forms it takes, are the main issues of contemporary political debate, especially in relatively developed societies. Experience shows that there can be many dysfunctional interventions. There is no consensus on the role of authorities, on when intervention is justified, or on what are constructive and destructive interventions in the wider context of present and future conditions.

The intervention which does seem to have consensus support is that of enforced compliance with existing social norms. It is beginning to become clear, however, that traditional preventive interventions by deterrent and punishment strategies are no longer effective. They do not deal with the sources of problems. So extensive have they become because of their failings that they are meeting resistance. Crime laws introduced by the United Kingdom in 1994 provoked public demonstrations protesting against infringements of freedoms and rights.

What is beginning to emerge is a realization by many members of societies as individuals, whether they are in support of the relatively privileged or of the underclass, that all are in a situation which in the longer term could turn out to be disastrous for them. The present is a critical stage in social evolution, requiring open and non-partisan discussion of the basic issues. This is a pre-condition of consensus change.

Probably the answer that will emerge through force of circumstances is more community activity in support of a community system as bottom-up decision-making becomes more significant in the light of local violence. As previously observed, it is only community services that can define this problem which is of such widespread social significance. The empirical evidence would suggest far more research is needed to see, for example, to what extent conditions in early childhood are correlated with subsequent behavioural problems, which give rise to leadership problems, management problems at the workplace, ethnicity conflicts and others. Human behaviour can no longer be ignored: the power political system and its deterrent strategies are on a course of self-destruction.

15

Holism

Opting out by authorities at any level because of complexities and competing ideologies is a policy of despair and potential disaster. This chapter is included to emphasize the need to treat as a totality the problems which societies face, and thus to get to their ultimate and common sources. It seeks to explain why treating problems as a whole does not add to complexities in analysis and in policy-making, but, on the contrary, helps to direct attention to core issues. It also helps in understanding the nature of a paradigm shift in thinking. The shift that this analysis suggests must take place is a shift from a power frame to a problem-solving one.

(This chapter may seem to divert from the theme of this Part, 'Towards consensus change', and to revert back to the introductory Part which sought to set out a frame of analysis. The concept of holism, however, is so central to problem-solving, as distinct from compliance processes, that it has been included in this Part as a backdrop to the following chapters.)

Twentieth-century trends in thinking and in policy-making

The strong tendency during this century has been towards specialization, both in policies and in thinking. Political ideologies and party platforms typically address particular issues and seek, thereby, to attract the support of special interest groups. Policies that are specific, however, can achieve their purposes only if formulated and pursued in the wider context of the total political, social and physical environment. Tackling a specific problem directly amounts to no more than treating symptoms and is more likely to help perpetuate the original problem. Equal rights legislation does not solve problems of gender, class and racial discrimination, although it may help particular individuals. Arms control does not abolish wars. A job creation policy is not a cure for a continuing problem of unemployment.

A second tendency has been to focus on the present and to brush aside concerns for even the short-term future. Societies are caught up in competitive trading relations. This requires the most efficient exploitation of resources. Scarce reserves of minerals, sources of energy, forests and other resources are exploited as fast as possible in order to maintain or improve balance of payments, employment and development generally. Current economic development is valued far more highly than present and future quality of life.

If there were to be a holistic approach to the problems of civilization, the policies advocated would be to decrease resource exploitation to sustainable levels and to satisfy the pressing physical needs of those in poverty by income redistribution nationally and internationally. Nevertheless, this is so far removed from political realities that it must be treated as an unreal observation. The practical reality is that contemporary economic systems will, in due course, inevitably lead to conditions that could no longer be defined as civilized, unless some drastic action is taken. This is likely only when these human cost consequences of systems are fully appreciated, and also when an alternative clear option is offered.

The academic community, in equating specialization with 'science', has sacrificed realities in order to be exact. But specialization has run into problems of complexity: the tactic has not worked. Gone are the exciting days of the 1960s and 1970s when statistics and computers led students in the social sciences to believe that at last scientific objectivity would lead to insights and to remedial policies never previously thought possible. Social sciences and political policies are both now under a cloud: conflicting empirical evidence, conflicting value systems, conflicting ideologies, have left societies without consensus philosophies or direction.

It is interesting that recent surveys suggest very strongly that the majority of citizens in developed countries seek quality of life, including security, rather than increased economic growth. They have little respect for economists, especially those who focus on investment and economic growth rather than on social concerns. The average citizen is more inclined to take a holistic view than the specialist in matters concerned with aspects of living.

Assessing the validity of the problem-solving frame

Is the analytical problem-solving conflict-resolution frame that takes into account behavioural dimensions one which is sufficiently comprehensive to point reliably to the types of changes that are required? Testing is the accepted scientific method by which to assess a proposal or an approach to a problem. There are, however, situations in which testing within a reasonable time period is not possible. Moreover, testing in the political and social sphere could be irrevocably dangerous if the premise or approach were false.

The quality of the approach, therefore, is the important consideration. This is certainly the case when the subject is an approach to change in political-social systems. First, the approach must get to the roots of specific problems, thereby revealing links between seemingly separate issues. It must point to the relevant system deficiencies, such as decision-making processes that lead to a lack of means to individual identity. These system deficiencies are, in turn, the common core sources of specific problems such as corruption, crime and violence. Second, the approach must lead to suggestions of appropriate policies that address these deficiencies. Third, it must point to processes by which this can be accepted. In short, an approach that is adequate must lead to the analysis of specific problems and appropriate policies in the context of the totality of political and social relationships.

To adopt such a generalist or holistic overview, cutting across various levels of society and specialized branches of knowledge, may seem to be unreasonably ambitious. But, on the contrary, standing back in this way, working from the general to the particular, provides a means of synthesis which itself facilitates perception of the particular. The sources of problems can be identified and appropriate measures taken to resolve them only if this diagnosis and treatment take place within a holistic frame. Specialization is a professional necessity, but it must be practised in the wider context of total situations and available knowledge.

Holism

Holism is a philosophy or a way of thinking that recognizes that the whole is greater than, and therefore different from, the sum of its parts. There are applied implications. In medicine, for example, holism would require the consideration of the whole person in the treatment of any specific symptoms and not just the treatment of these symptoms.

In a particular conflict situation there is a large number of parts. In an analysis of the causes of the war with Iraq in 1992 these parts would have included leadership and ethnicity problems, relations with neighbours, the complex motivations of intervening powers and many others. So also with domestic violence and even with a confined inter-personal conflict. But just listing and even considering all variables as separate issues would still not give an accurate and agreed definition of the total situation, or a clear policy approach to it – as was, indeed, the case with the Iraq war. An explanation that includes and also relates the separate issues is required.

It is this need for a comprehensive or holistic approach that challenges reporters and historians. They have to select what appear to be the main events and data during a given period and to interpret them so as to present an integrated account of behaviours and events. Selections and interpretations are finally based on the limited evidence available and, significantly, on the political and social orientations of the reporter or historian. To others, who have lived through or are interested in the same period, the interpretation of the selected parts rarely seems to give an accurate picture of the whole.

Indeed, it may give a totally different picture, depending on the selection and interpretation of the data.

This is the process of inductive reasoning – a process by which a general conclusion is arrived at after gathering evidence based on experience and on experimental or selected data. Inductive reasoning is the traditional thought process. It is followed by decision-makers and most scholars. It is how most people operate every day in their lives.

Holism provides a different approach and methodology. It is one that is deductive – a process of reasoning by which interpretations of data and conclusions are arrived at on the basis of some previously stated general theory or premises. It is the theory, not selection of data, which is the focus of analytical attention. It supplies the comprehensive explanatory frame in which to analyse a specific problem. There is little reliance on selected and detailed data, and subjectivity in interpretation is therefore transferred to the original premises.

It needs to be noted, however, that a deductive frame also has elements of 'abduction', to use a C. S. Peirce term.[1] Abduction refers to the guessing element in theory development and premises, and the errors that are possible in deducing. In a deductive process the explanatory frame replaces selected data as the possible major source of error. A deductive approach is, therefore, more reliable than an inductive one only if the theoretical frame employed is adequate and valid. This points to the need for theory application to be monitored continuously and for suitable policy adjustments to be made.

The power frame

The traditional Western frame of political analysis has been and still is 'power politics' based on a theory of human aggressiveness. Given the power, aggressive tactics will be pursued.

While based on selected empirical evidence, it could nevertheless be that this power frame meets theoretical requirements and should be regarded as being as valid as any that might be arrived at deductively. In short, an analytical interpretation of the totality of human behaviour could lead to a theory no different from that arrived at by empirical evidence drawn from selected data. It is necessary, therefore, to examine this power frame before rejecting it and suggesting an alternative.

History has usually been interpreted within the power frame. The relative economic and military power of nations has been used to explain relationships and foreign policies. The power theory is also used as an explanatory frame in which to analyse internal political relations. It is extended to explain problems which authorities face, thus justifying the use of coercive power as a means of control.

Power theories assume, as has been argued, that the person is unimportant in the sense that the person or group can be coerced into behaviours required to maintain institutions and social norms. The belief leads to government by dominant interests in accordance with the relative power or influence of those interests. It leads, also, to the least possible intervention by authorities, except that required to ensure that social and economic behaviours accord with the norms established by these interests. The political, social and economic consequences of such practice must be the adversarial institutions and relationships that characterize traditional elite-dominated societies. These are a major source of conflicts.

As a policy frame power politics is understandable. If a person, an organization, a country, has power, it will use that power to try to achieve its purposes. But as an explanatory frame it has pushed other influences, such as behavioural influences, into the background. It fails as a theoretical frame because it is too limited.

'Power politics' was finally faulted even as a policy frame when it was discovered in the cases of North Korea and Vietnam that deterrence does not deter when there are at stake independence issues and related human needs, rather than just negotiable interests. If this had been deduced and anticipated from a more comprehensive frame, it would have avoided costly defeats in wars.

The absence of holism

Decision-makers, administrators and thinkers generally are not skilled at standing back and seeing their particular concerns in the broad picture of social relationships, of the environment and of time. Indeed, their specialized locations in professions, disciplines and administrations determine their limited focus.

There is a flow of books reflecting concern with the crisis in civilizations, especially in the United States which is experiencing a decline in its power position, including an inability to contain dissident behaviours. Arthur Schlesinger has made clear his concerns about growing racial conflicts in his *The Disuniting of America: Reflections on a Multicultural Society*.[2] The same theme is taken up by Cornel West in his *Race Matters*.[3] Chomsky in his *Year 501: The Conquest Continues*,[4] and his *Deterring Democracy*,[5] pursues the theme of Jonathan Kwitny a decade earlier in his *Endless Enemies: The Making of an Unfriendly World. How America's Worldwide Interventions Destroy Democracy and Free Enterprise and Defeat our own Best Interests*.[6] Robert Reich has pointed to the adverse implications for American workers of the growing global economy which is now dominated by corporations which take advantage of cheap labour in underdeveloped countries in his *The Work of Nations*.[7] Each has his own important concern. But there is no central theme. No policy remedies emerge.

Neil Postman in his *Technopoly* points out that education within a classroom group is swinging to technical and computer education, at the expense of communication and thinking.[8] By focusing on the dangers of a limited education he may be getting closer to a general explanation of problems societies face and their inability to prevent and to resolve them. The breaking down of knowledge in the name of science is probably a significant reason for humanity's persistent failure to control its destiny. But there is still no general explanation or theory to be included in education which would guide institutional change.

In contemporary societies people generally have to pursue their special interests. As a consequence they tend to perceive situations in a limited context, to seek limited remedies for problems and generally to reduce seemingly complex variables to simple propositions. As a consequence there has been a strong tendency to attribute blame or cause to the individuals immediately concerned, rather than to the totality of circumstances that led to the problems. This appeals, of course, to the majority of more privileged peoples who understandably feel that many social problems are due, not to system deficiencies, but to individual lack of social values and social responsibility.

Diagnosis has become a matter of chance, depending on the interest areas of those making it. A psychologist makes one, a sociologist another, politicians yet others according to their specific knowledge and interests. Limited ideologies and belief systems influence all. This lack of a holistic view obviously leads to superficial, false and often damaging policy decisions.

Culture

An analytical approach to social problems that delves deeply into the nature of relationship and system problems cuts across ideologies and thought systems. It follows that it also cuts across cultures, or any other sources of preconceptions. In this behavioural approach, therefore, an attempt is made to delve deeper than culture and to treat cultural differences as differences in method or means in achieving human needs and social cohesion rather than differences in objectives. Major religious movements which currently employ violence to promote their interests may have sources as much in the past history of colonialism as they do in religious beliefs.

It is important in the analytical process to discover the difference between goals and means. Goals are held in common. One such goal is the satisfaction of inherent human needs that are shared across cultures. But there are many different means by which personal security, recognition and identity can be achieved. While people cannot tolerate the denial of their needs, different means of fulfilling those needs might be found in different cases. Demands for autonomy within nation-states, for example, seem at first sight to be demands for sovereignty in the traditional sense. Further analysis, however, might bring to the surface desires for close functional relationships with other minorities and lead to innovative options that might bypass the issue of sovereignty.

Ideological differences

It is possible to eliminate biases and differences of opinion by digging deeper into behavioural relationships. The political 'Left' and 'Right' may differ on why specific problems exist and what to do about them, but both express the same concerns for the present and fears for the future. In July 1992 the liberal US journal, *The Nation*, led with the observation that 'It is very easy to discuss *what* has gone wrong. It is not so easy to discuss what should be done to correct what has gone wrong. It is absolutely impossible in our public discussion to discuss *why* so much has gone wrong.' Instead of in-depth analysis there are ideological and value-oriented explanations which reflect to a large degree the immediate interests of those concerned. Ideological beliefs and values are a fall-back position taken when there are unresolved problems in social relationships. Ideology need not be an issue when there is a searching analysis of relationship problems.

Questioning of assumptions

In a holistic approach it is necessary to question assumptions that have traditionally been widely accepted, especially assumptions that concern individual conformity with social norms. This approach should, for example, extend even to questioning the social validity and viability of the traditional concept of majority government on which parliaments and congresses are based. Faced with problems experienced by young people, with entrenched class and cultural differences, with the presence of ethnic minorities within nation-states, such fundamental questioning is now unavoidable if creative options are to be found.

One of the most supported research areas during the Cold War was strategic studies. This was a research area that was encouraged by governments and was a direct product of balance-of-power theories. It was based on the assumption that deterrence deters. Such studies persisted even though a major world power was militarily defeated or frustrated in Vietnam, Korea and elsewhere. In relation to violence and crime, also, the deterrence assumption has been faulted.

In the immediate post-Second World War period, movements for independence from colonial domination were regarded with suspicion – Soviet and Chinese communism was considered to be responsible for them. In addition independence was regarded as an undesirable trend from the point-of-view of the interests of many of the inhabitants of colonial territories: they would be better off under colonialism. Similarly, in the contemporary world, integration is assumed to be more desirable than 'disintegration'. Yet this negative can be transformed into a positive, such as the establishment of autonomies with close and harmonious functional relationships. History is a record of amalgamations and separations of political and geographical units. Yet the assumption carries with it a value orientation: the one is good, the other bad, leading to definitions of those who are the 'guilty' parties in a particular boundary or ethnic conflict.

Some of the most widely held, yet possibly false, assumptions that arise out of the institutional or power frame are in the area of economics. One assumption, previously referred to, is that subsidies and tariffs are to be avoided so as to promote the most efficient use of resources. There are cultural reasons why a society should offer a diversity of employment, rather than be wholly dependent on agriculture, mining or some other primary enterprises. There is no reason why a society should not decide that it is in its short- and long-term interests to have industries that would not be possible in conditions of free trade. It seems, in fact, that this almost moral objection to tariffs and subsidies is one being imposed by the larger economies which have developed as a result of such protection, but which now wish to ensure that other markets are open to them.

Questioning of assumptions is important, but in itself it is a negative exercise, perhaps leading to the conclusion that complexities are such that no positive solutions can ever be discovered, or even exist. Questioning becomes positive when it leads to reformulations of theory and greater insights into human behaviours. Questioning is only the beginning of an analysis.

New concepts and problems of language

There is usually difficulty, or at least serious delay, in adjusting concepts – and, therefore, institutions and practices – to altered circumstances. Take the concept of the nation-state. Power has in the past been associated with the military and economic influence of the centrally controlled nation-state. Power balances were regarded as the means by which wars between them could be avoided. In recent decades forced and voluntary migrations have taken place and now few states are mono-ethnic. The global society is no longer one comprised of fifty or so largely mono-ethnic nation-states dominated by a few more powerful states, but of large numbers of social units which have attained or are seeking some form of independence and international recognition. Yet the nation-state concept remains. There has been a lag in comprehending the irrelevance of power politics and power balances which are the expression of nation-states.

Concepts, such as power and the nation-state, must be subject to change as conditions change. If institutions change as the result of boundary and population changes, of alterations in productive processes and of all the other influences that affect societies over time, and if institutions cannot be maintained through the exercise of power, then conceptual thinking has to change if there is to be an understanding of the problems of societies.

A different approach and the consequent use of altered concepts requires a different language. Within a traditional power or coercive frame, 'solving' the problem of street violence could mean allocating more police for street duties. Problem-solving within a conflict resolution context has a quite different meaning. Getting at the roots of a problem and eliminating sources of conflict reflects a different philosophy and requires a different term, which is the reason for introducing 'provention'.[9]

A holistic approach thus opens up new areas of thinking, different approaches to social problems and altered concepts. It requires either new terms or giving new meaning to terms in general use. Challenging, yes, but also rewarding. The conceptual shift in thinking promoted by a holistic approach provokes thinking about both theories and policies.

Notes

1   See C. S. Peirce, *The Essentials of Peirce*, ed. N. Houser and C. Kloesel (Bloomington, Indiana University Press, 1992).

2   A. M. Schlesinger, *The Disuniting of America: Reflections on a Multicultural Society* (New York, Norton and Co., 1992).

3   C. West, *Race Matters* (Boston, Beacon Press, 1993).

4   N. Chomsky, *Year 501: The Conquest Continues* (Boston, South End Press, 1993).

5   N. Chomsky, *Deterring Democracy* (New York, Hill and Wang, 1991).

6   J. Kwitny, *Endless Enemies: The Making of an Unfriendly World* (New York, Congdon and Weed, 1984).

7   R. Reich, *The Work of Nations* (New York, Vintage Press, 1992).

8   N. Postman, *Technopoly: The Surrender of Culture to Technology* (New York, Vintage Press, 1993).

9   J. Burton, *Conflict: Resolution and Provention* (New York, St Martin's Press and London, Macmillan, 1990).

16

Bottom-up decision-making

A decade or so ago there were some scholars who were regarded as being on the fringe when writing about *Beyond Adversary Democracy*.[1] They were pointing out the advantages of face-to-face community decision-making as the means of dealing with pressing personal and social problems. There were others who reacted against rationality, as they saw it, in large bureaucratic organizations, arguing that this was destructive of democracy which required tentative decision-making, especially at a community level. Hierarchical and centralized power is impervious to criticisms that would be made if there were an awareness of conditions of living. What was required was *Discursive Democracy*.[2] In 1992 an insightful collection of papers appeared with the title, *Putting Power in its Place: Create Community Control*. It was argued that an inevitable consequence of central decision-making is that 'decisions are made that do not take into account the knowledge that can only come from knowing a place through years, indeed generations, of inhabitation ... At issue is finding a way to shift the power back home where the possibility for democratic and ecological integrity lies. And the urgency is to do so before we find ourselves to be the powerless, feudalized peasantry of the transnational corporations.'[3] If a human needs element is to be included in decision-making, then it may be that there must be far less top-down decision-making, and far more community administration and policy-making.

Community government

The top-down approach is comprised of central authorities and regional and local governments with specific functions. Local government is usually merely an administrative arm of a central authority, having responsibilities for local services. Typically it lacks direct community contact despite its local activities. Indeed, the tendency under economic rationalism is for local authorities, for example 'states', to reduce the number of local councils, thus extending their regions and lessening even further direct community contact.

In practice, it is community-based authorities that are in the best position to introduce the required human perspective to social issues. By community is meant ten thousand or so teenagers and adults. It is at this level that specific problems can be identified and treated, perhaps initially in only a band-aid way, but in a way that alerts authorities at a macro and financial level, through local representatives of central legislature, to the emergence and the nature of social problems.

Decision-making at a community level is likely to focus on human needs as they surface in family, social and school environments. It is likely to be, therefore, more problem-solving than would be the case at a level at which there is little face-to-face contact between decision-makers and those affected. The administration of schools and teacher–pupil relationships can best be promoted at this level.

In privileged areas community organizations are likely to focus primarily on security. There is, however, a strong incentive to help promote development in neighbouring regions which are the source of insecurity. In South Africa, with the assistance of an external facilitating body, a wealthy white district made major contributions to a neighbouring black squatter camp which was both a source of important services and a threat to security. This is an extreme case, but the same applies in principle to regions in which there are privileged and underprivileged in neighbouring districts. The more the social barriers can be broken down, the better for all concerned.

It is from this level that insights can be deduced into the sources of major national and international violence and crime, problems of competing leaderships and others. Discovering sources or causes of problems was the starting point of this analysis. Sources are deduced from an adequate analysis and theory of human behaviour. It is at this community level that empirical evidence is observable, and it is at this micro level that theory can be developed and applied at a macro level.

The psychology of community co-operation

For some it is by work-related activities and relationships that individual identity needs are fully satisfied. For the majority of members of a society, however, these relationships are of limited value: other activities are found, including identifications in sports, in party politics, in ethnicity, in support for the local school or church, in participation in voluntary organizations, and in many other ways.

Community identification is especially in evidence where there is a shared social environment, for example where there is only one major source of employment, such as a local mining or a major manufacturing industry. When societies were smaller and more integrated, such community identification played, as did tribal relationships, a major role in the maintenance of social

135

norms. This remains an important influence in agricultural regions where, despite being in a competitive market, there is extensive social and production-related co-operation at a community level.

Industrial societies are usually no longer of this community type. Communications and available means of transport have made housing areas no more than residences, relationships being pursued over long distances. This is especially the case where women work and are no longer at home to foster community contacts. With increased mobility of labour, increased transport and communications and increased home entertainments, more often than not neighbours have little contact. If there are problems there is a hot line to the police. Public education and health receives limited support from the community. The functional need for close and harmonious relationships that is a feature of isolated agricultural communities does not seem to influence behaviours in the modern and crowded city, nor even in suburbs. One possible exception is limited community involvement in schools.

Yet it is at this community level that most crime and violence occurs. While central authorities and their agencies must deal with external threats to security and organized major crime within their boundaries, it is at the community level that some of the main social problems that lead to violence and crime have their social source.

As a consequence there are all manner of tensions, disputes and conflicts within communities that are experienced at the local community level. But decision-makers at the national level, concerned with law-making, policing and finances, cannot define and identify them. Authorities are aware of violence and crime and of the costs of policing and control, but not of their sources. Teenage unemployment of 30 or 40 per cent, which is usual if the national employment figure is about 10 per cent, is a politically disturbing statistic, but in personal and social terms conveys little to decision-makers concerned with financial policies.

Nor are authorities sufficiently aware of the positive aspects of community relationships. Both voluntary and official community involvement and decision-making have immediate role and identity benefits for those involved. They could be an important part of education and social development for adults as well as children.

In societies as they have now emerged as part of the global society, the role of central authorities within a problem-solving frame probably would be to give far more decision-making and administrative responsibilities to community-located organizations and governments. Community participation in decision-making within educational and health institutions, in policing, in communications, in recreations and all the other activities that are community shared would be better informed and more problem-solving, and also have positive side-effects in community relationships.

Such local or community legislatures, formal or informal, voluntary or compulsory, have not received serious attention in political theory or practice, despite an important literature on 'Communitarianism'.[4] Such community government has not developed significantly within the traditional state system. While many religious and social organizations act as lobby groups in respect of particular value systems or interests, communities concerned with the full range of social problems have not had influence on matters of social policy. The possibilities of community-based government do not come into courses on political philosophy. Yet it may well be that it is here that there is a gap to be filled if problems of alienation and the sources of crime, trivial and major, are to be detected and defined at source. It is at this level that detailed applied research is possible that would reveal the nature of ethnic conflict, street gangs, street violence and crime. It is at this level that intervention and assistance can be most effective.

The forms such an authority could take are obviously many. They could range from elected assemblies to the encouragement by various means of voluntary community organizations with which the local member of the central authority would work. The point to be made is that in a global system in which national authorities are affected by conditions over which they have little or no control, communities must take initiatives to deal with consequential problems.

Unfortunately those who have been advocating community decision-making have regarded this as a substitute for central authorities. The two must be married. Community experiences, opinion and activities can be the important source of information on which central authorities can act. In the party political system representatives rely mostly on their local party organizations for contacts with their electorate. If electorates were divided into communities of ten thousand or so citizens there would be a reduction in party and ideological confrontations. Representatives could get a far better sense of consensus views and sources of problems than is usually possible. A bottom-up decision-making process would not replace the top-down process, but it would change it so that it would act far more as an informed co-ordinator.

Community government and corporate bodies

Such an emphasis on community-based decision-making is logical within the emerging global system and within the problem-solving frame in which it has been analysed. In a power frame systems and decision-making trickle down from the top, as argued above. There are 'great powers' at the international level, central authorities at the nation-state level at which minorities must conform, authoritative systems throughout the society down to family relationships. In a problem-solving frame and in conditions in which economic and related conditions cannot be controlled, the opposite is the case. Reference has been made to the obvious need for corporate–state co-operation in devising and applying policies that can deal with an alientated 20 per cent of the population of any industrial society, which is a major source of problems that are threatening quality of life generally. Experience in the United States is that the message has not yet got through to the more privileged and to special interest groups (such as the gun lobby) that the emerging corporate system is creating conditions of violence which will in due course threaten the haves as well as the have-nots. Legislation to deal with crime, especially provisions for welfare assistance, or to deal with health in a comprehensive way, is impossible without leadership from within this industrial section of the society sufficient to offset lobby influences. It is the corporate system that has the capacity and an interest in looking to the future. Without this corporate support no national government, liberal or conservative, can pursue the required policies. Even with such co-operation, there remains the problem of competitiveness which limits the possibilities of maintaining quality of life in the absence of far greater community responsibilities, especially in education and in social relationships generally, including family cohesion and child development. This is the structural context in which institutions of government need to be reassessed. Community influences would bring to the attention of special interest groups far more their self-interests in co-operating with government in dealing with welfare and education problems, especially of the alienated 20 per cent.

This all has the ring of wishful thinking. This is, however, largely because bottom-up decision-making is so far removed from contemporary practice. Circumstances are forcing trends in this direction, but unfortunately towards state government responsibilities rather than local communities. State governments are as far removed from experienced realities as are federal governments. If thought were given to alternative structures, bottom-up decision-making could emerge as a practical option. For example, local representatives of legislatures could be provided with funding necessary to organize community services and community investigations into local problems, in addition to community meetings in place of their local party support groups. Some experiments are needed, also some assessments of movements in this direction which are taking place in countries like South Africa where the problems of violence make such initiatives essential.[5]

Notes

1 J. Mansbridge, *Beyond Adversary Democracy* (New York, Basic Books, 1980).
2 J. S. Dryzek, *Discursive Democracy* (Cambridge, Cambridge University Press, 1990).
3 J. Plant and C. Plant, eds, *Putting Power in its Place: Create Community Control* (Philadelphia PA, New Society Publishers, 1992).
4 A. Etzioni, *The Spirit of Community: Rights, Responsibilities and the Communitarian Agenda* (New York, Crown Publishers, 1993).

5   See *Track Two* (Rondebosch, Journal of the Centre for Conflict Resolution), 4: 4
      (December 1995) and 5: 1 (March 1996).

17

Education and consensus

In this analysis there has been a stress on the need for holistic approaches, that is, defining specific problems in the context of the totality of all other problems and of living conditions generally. Change that gets to the roots of problems must be comprehensive in this sense, touching all levels of societies and all aspects of relationships. Societies are a totality: behaviour anywhere affects behaviour everywhere. A local denial of identity, for example through unemployment, relates to domestic violence and crime. Power struggles involving wars have environmental and social effects. Problems in the home and at school result in anti-social behaviours years later.

Ultimately societies must, in their search for a solution to their pressing problems of survival, look to education and other consensus means of bringing about change, and in this way influence and support institutions and policies. If there is to be social stability along with change, there must be a public awareness of the sources of problems and a consensus approach to social solutions.

Fortunately, both awareness and learning are increasing rapidly in contemporary conditions of communications, including television documentaries, talk-back radio programmes, the various forms of the published media and the growing direct communication through personal computers. Not only are victims of violence able to give their versions, but so too are those who have been violent. Very revealing publications are available.[1]

Education is, however, a very long-term process. Change is urgent in many areas of concern. There is a need for short-cuts. First, there are important changes that can be made in legislatures, law and business systems without constitutional and public processes, changes that would be widely welcomed, such as fundamentally altering legislative procedures so as to transform adversarial debate into creative analysis of problems. Such a change would set an example for social systems generally. Second, the discussion and publication of the nature and implications of problem-solving processes give opportunities to administrators in all institutions and systems to avoid the costly confrontations that occur in adversarial and authoritative systems.

The need for fundamental and comprehensive solutions

It needs to be stressed, however, that a problem-solving option needs to be more than a band-aid dealing with a particular problem within a particular institution. Political and social problems have been dealt with in the past largely by measures that deal only with their symptoms. Fundamental systems failures, leading to social strife, have frequently brought only changes in political leaderships or political parties, which in most cases changed little or nothing. Ethnic conflicts have led to coups and military dictatorships that do no more than temporarily suppress conflict. Widespread dissatisfaction with social conditions has led to revolutions resulting in quite different types of systems, but with similar problems. Changes in leaderships and modifications in systems have usually been desperate and unplanned responses lacking an adequate explanation of the original failures and the sources of desperation. Communism was exceptional in that it was a planned process, but it lacked provisions for processes of change to cope with conditions that subsequently emerged or were not initially taken into account.

Remedies attempted at other political and social levels have equally been directed towards the immediate symptoms of a specific problem: school violence has led to containment measures, strikes to altered work practices or higher wages and mass lay-offs, street violence to altered police routines, sex and racial discriminations to changes in laws and regulations, domestic violence to the introduction of reporting systems, and so on.

Just simple costing shows the need to go further than token *ad hoc* policies. The Australian Institute of Criminology has estimated that the annual cost of crime in Australia is between A$17 and A$27 billion. Detailed regional studies revealed links between unemployment and 87 per cent of crime. Yet the Australian government in 1994 proposed spending only A$1 billion a year on a jobs programme to deal with 10 per cent unemployment. Statistical assessments can be made that suggest that there are causal relationships between separate issue areas; but these connections have usually been ignored. Higher public expenditure on education, reductions in income inequalities, and many other such changes in budget policies would be suggested as *cost savings* by a more holistic analysis of specific social problems.

The essence of consensus

To achieve longer-term stability a popular consensus is necessary. Little thought, however, has been given to legislative and decision-making processes by which widespread agreement can be achieved at any political or social level. Means to consensus have not been of interest in the power frame, which assumes that minorities must adjust to the decisions of authorities.

If there were to be consensus change there would have to be processes that were neutral ideologically, and arrived at after a cost analysis of change and its consequences made by all sections of the society. Material interests, and wider human interests at a personal and community level, would need to be satisfied to a degree which was declared acceptable, given circumstances and practical possibilities, by affected groups.

Not only is majority government far removed from consensus rule, but it reflects conflict between interests, usually material interests, which tend to ignore behavioural sources of social alienation and conflict. As Postman has observed, language, such as the use of the term 'democracy', can readily become an ideology employed to justify a position, regardless of lack of electoral support.[2]

Nor could any planned society meet the consensus requirement, for the planning would have to be so comprehensive that it met all the major requirements of all sections of society today and tomorrow. Such planning would require an effective and dedicated bureaucracy. Bureaucracies are, on the contrary, 'a co-ordinated series of techniques for reducing the amount of information that requires processing'.[3] By their nature they could not perform such a task.

The search is for some continuing process that is designed to make administration more efficient in moving beyond the traditional goal of establishing a secure society by social and legal norms which is frequently at the expense of human aspirations. There is the need to build into institutions, all institutions – legislatures, industry, the local community, the family, the school, the hospital, the police force and all others – regular means of reassessment that link the present to the future, rather than just the past to the present, as is more usually the case. A form of regular and professional auditing for social and behavioural purposes is probably more important than the provision of minimum wages in assuring quality of life.

In modern participatory societies there is a serious dilemma. While public opinion provides a social consensus view beyond which authorities cannot move without losing support, it is not always well informed on means to ends or free of ideological prejudices. Scientists and scholars generally can exercise some influence in bringing to attention present and future issues of social concern. Writers of fiction, artists and many others have a role to play in suggesting alternative views. Most important, however, are movements for change that emerge out of social concerns and which are led usually by relatively informed persons perhaps motivated by some particular interest and commitment.[4] There probably is, in democracies, a need for an 'upper house' that has for its electorate the whole nation rather than regions or separate states, thus giving opportunities for representation to special groups such as those concerned with the environment, gender problems, ethnic minorities, the underclass, young people and others.

Facilitators

A first step is to promote a general awareness of problem-solving processes as an alternative to coercion and power politics. This requires a reassessment of educational programmes at all levels, from kindergarten to university. This has only just begun to happen. There is now a library on conflict prevention and resolution, but, though there are now some examples,[5] these yet have to be translated into readable and teaching material and made widely available. There is an urgent need for more published guides within the alternative problem-solving frame for public decision-makers and administrators, industrial managers and unions, teachers at all levels, parents, social workers, probation officers, judges, police, the defence services, foreign offices and all who have special roles within the social system, and who would be helped by a specific translation of problem-solving processes that applied to their areas of concern and interest.

A second step is to ensure that facilitators who can assist in the processes of change are available. There are many universities with degree courses in conflict resolution and which prepare already experienced people for a more effective role in industry, local government and other occupational fields. More resources need to be directed towards this growing profession.

Education and consensus change

A consensus shift away from a power frame to a problem-solving one must, as has been said, depend finally on education. Education, in turn, will not shift its focus until there is the necessary questioning of basic assumptions in every social discipline. This can only be a long-term phenomenon. Present trends in education are in the opposite direction.

In his important book, referred to previously, Neil Postman points out how education has, step-by-step, moved away from how to think and towards technological skills. This movement is promoted by the availability of computers in schools. Universities are tending to become technological institutions as the perception spreads that specialized qualifications are more likely to lead to employment opportunities. This takes one step further the tendency even in university education for 'scientific method' to exclude holistic approaches that include consideration of human dimensions.

The trend towards technological education is understandable and probably desirable as technology invades the workplace. But there is no reason why technology should replace training in how to think, to question and to conceptualize. There is no reason why education at all levels should not include training in what is obviously the most important subject for human beings, the essence of human relationships, and how they are to be developed in the future.

We have seen how a human dimension is surfacing and it is threatening all social systems. Technology can help by providing sophisticated security measures. Indeed, for many it is now possible, and this will be more general in the future, to work and to shop from home, to have entertainment and 'virtual reality' provided by new technologies. In terms of human needs, however, this is not the way forward for civilizations in crisis. It forecasts the demise of civilizations.

The social importance of a questioning education

A questioning education has become more and not less important with technological developments. People, young and old, are brought up in the adversarial systems that have been described. Their practical education is in we–they relationships and how to win. Even the majority of sports and recreations are learning experiences within this frame. There is no consensus knowledge in any Western society of possible alternatives to adversarial relationships.

The consequence is that which has been observed in previous chapters. Leaderships bring adversarial approaches to their problems. Peoples living in democracies give their support to aggressive leaders and to aggressive behaviours in the marketplace. But the institutions that have evolved over time and which have their origins in adversarial relationships must be self-destructive unless they can be conditioned and controlled so as to lead to collaborative behaviours in dealing with social and environmental problems. Collaborative behaviours imply an ability to be analytical, to question, to understand other viewpoints, to get to the core of problems. If education systems deny training in such arts they are contributing to the crisis in civilizations, no matter how much technology they make available.

There are many publications that look *Beyond Self-Interest*[6] and which raise fundamental questions that need to be in the minds of decision-makers, who are prone to be influenced more by pressure groups than by their perceptions of social interests. But these are publications aimed at advocacy rather than educators. Reports coming out of France claim that 'France is still the only country in the world that requires the study of philosophy in high school.' Some 570,000 high school students must show they can handle abstract issues.[7] By philosophy is meant more than the history of philosophy or the thinking of past philosophers. What is meant is how to think, how to question, how to be analytical, how to be conceptual and holistic in thinking about problems.

144

Education: a political throw-away

In immediate political terms, education, along with health and the environment, tends to become of secondary importance when interest groups resist tax increases, especially in recessions. In most societies public education expenditures per head are tending to decrease, despite the increases in knowledge to be absorbed and the greater complexities of industrial processes. More and more, education, especially higher education, becomes confined to higher income groups. The further alienation of others follows.

An inheritance of class has influenced the educational system and its priorities. There has been an educated class and there have been others who were expected to perform menial tasks. If societies are to seek to promote democratic institutions, based on consensus values and beliefs, a much more broadly based education will be required. Whether the focus is on the workplace or on democratic processes, or on ways of reducing alienation and crime, education becomes the core influence. The message has yet to get through to those on higher incomes that it is greatly in their interests to contribute through taxation to an increasing educational budget. 'Beyond self-interest' is in reality rapidly becoming the essence of self-interest.

A defensive answer is that this argument does not sufficiently take into account differences in levels of intelligence and the inability of some races and the 'underclass' to achieve academically. The empirical evidence is that measures of intelligence alter with opportunities.

A viable option

A focus on the longer term by relying on education as a solution to the problems of societies and the global system is not necessarily as depressing as it might seem. The option of problem-solving conflict resolution as a political philosophy to take the place of the traditional power politics frame is a recent discovery. Its underlying theory argues that there are inherent human needs of security, identity and recognition to be satisfied and that institutions must adjust to the satisfaction of such needs rather than the other way around. Articulated only in recent decades this alternative to tradition is viable and an asset of unprecedented significance.

Civilizations are in crisis. The costs of the present, including personal security, are being experienced by even the most privileged. Change, once conceptualized as insecurity, is at last likely to be regarded as rather the cornerstone of security. Education is the most reliable means of change.

Notes

1   For example, D. Prothrow-Smith with M. Weissman, *Deadly Consequences: How*

Violence is Destroying our Teenage Population and a Plan to Begin Solving the Problem (New York, Harper Perennial, 1991).

2 N. Postman, *Technopoly: The Surrender of Culture to Technology* (New York, Vintage Press, 1993), p. 123.

3 Ibid., p. 84.

4 See, for example, R. Rubenstein and associates, *Frameworks for Interpreting Conflict: A Handbook for Journalists, Institute for Conflict Analysis and Resolution* (George Mason University, Virginia, Report No. 2). G. Tillett, *Resolving Conflict: A Practical Approach* (Sydney, Sydney University Press, 1991).

5 See V. Burgmann, *Power and Protest: Movements of Change in Australian Society* (Sydney, Allen and Unwin, 1993).

6 J. Mansbridge, ed., *Beyond Self Interest* (Chicago, University of Chicago Press, 1990).

7 A. Riding, *New York Times* (7 July 1994).

18

Conclusions

An examination of contemporary institutions confirms that there remain in societies, as was the case in earlier philosophers' utopias, those who claim the right to determine social behaviours and expect obedience, and others who are expected to conform. In this sense all institutions, including often the family, still remain adversarial in structure, even though the governed sometimes accept their lot.

There have, however, been significant changes in the composition of, and relations between, these divisions in societies. In practice, 'have-nots' and 'haves' can no longer be defined by reference to capital and labour or management and labour. In developed countries an upper and middle class combine both resource ownerships, management, professionals and skilled workers. It is they who are represented in political parties. Indeed, it is now frequently difficult to separate 'Right' and 'Left' in party politics. Both accept inequalities and both resist the tax increases necessary to support comprehensive social, health and educational services.

While relationships at management level could still be improved greatly, the serious structural confrontation that persists is in relations between managers and skilled workers in industry on the one side and routine workers and the unemployed on the other. In short, at the ground level there has been a shift from capital versus labour to those who happen to have made it versus those who are no longer part of the system.

The dominant middle-class section of a developed country is reluctant to admit the existence of the prevailing 20 per cent alienation problem. It is they who stand in the way of bringing this population back into the system. In industrially developed countries the norm is the promotion of the interests of organized labour and capital, and the neglect of the alienated 20 per cent, which includes many young people who do not have a role in the system. Despite this change in industrial relations, legislatures remain adversarial in character, still reflecting early labour struggles versus resource ownership, leading to government and opposition on policies even though there are no longer major ideological or interest differences. The result is a continuing absence of any problem-solving orientation.

Nor does the academic community seem to have shifted from the basic hypotheses of early utopian thinking, or to have assessed the full implications of traditional institutions in altered global circumstances. J. K. Galbraith observes how many economists 'play to the contented', how the market society prejudices longer-term considerations and how the creation of an 'underclass' ensures costly social disorder.[1]

The 20 per cent problem

It is still thought that the relevant policy in respect of this 20 per cent problem is to promote investment and growth. At the same time, it is feared that inflation would result from high levels of employment and increased borrowing so increased interest rates are relied upon to dampen growth, thus countervailing investment as an employment policy. While such control is now, in any case, beyond the capacities of national governments, alternatives have not emerged in the present system. The 20 per cent problem remains as an irrelevant political issue except to the extent that additional police and gaols are required. There is a lot of costing still to be done by those who resist investing in quality of life.

'Goodbye to Great Britain' is the title of an article written in 1994 by an Australian journalist who compared Great Britain in 1954 with a Great Britain of forty years later.[2] He described the increasing levels of crime and insecurity, the obvious poverty and the continuing deterioration in education and health services. He observed that, despite this, the rich continued to get richer. The same stories are coming out of most developed countries. The United States is a special case. In 1987 average homicide rates for young men in developed countries in Europe and elsewhere were two or three per 100,000 men. In the United States they were twenty-two. While the availability of guns and racial tensions contributed to this difference, analysis shows that the main cause was relative poverty.[3] Within a human needs frame it could be deduced that within poverty there is a lack of role and identity.

As already argued, within the party political power frame such trends must be expected. Government controlled by a party representing business interests and the more wealthy, tends to cut taxes, making it necessary to cut expenditures on social services and infrastructures. It deregulates the economy, leaving the market to make the primary decisions as to income distribution. Short-term political expediency is the guide to policies. Future generations and the environment are given a low priority. Increased police controls and gaols become the means of dealing with the consequences. Longer-term consequences of ignoring the 20 per cent problem are brushed aside, being too challenging politically to deal with.

Thus a vacuum has developed: in traditional thinking, emerging out of traditional institutions, there are no viable policies that could induce consent. The vacuum tends to be filled by those who have special and limited goals: environmental, full employment, improved education, equal opportunities and others of this kind. All are important, but when advocated separately as though each were the core problem, an element of fanaticism is inevitable, giving rise to reasonable oppositions. These separate endeavours are not a substitute for comprehensive policies that emerge out of a holistic analysis which seeks to identify the common underlying sources of these separate problems.

The search for an option

One of the difficulties in formulating policies has been to define the problem of violence and crime. At the level of law and order it is a police problem, and generally speaking middle-class electorates understand this definition and support its consequential policies. Amnesty International points to violations of human rights as the source of violence.[4] At the workplace, which is the site of a sixth of crime in the United States, it is a management problem.[5] At the school level it is a discipline problem accompanied by inadequate teaching and facilities and attempts to cover up the incidence of violence.[6] At the social and family levels it is an adjustment problem, requiring counselling, education and recreation diversions so that there can be a redirection of anger away from others.[7] If societies are to deal with conflict, violence and crime at its sources, the institution of the family is probably the main one which requires attention. The probability is that a great deal of conflict, violence and crime can be traced to early childhood. Whether it is serial killings, killings in ethnic conflicts by military regimes, repressive administrations, ruthless management or child abuse by teachers and official custodians, the sources can frequently be traced to early child control and perhaps abuse of those responsible for this control.

These are all definitions and treatments dealing only with symptoms of the more fundamental human needs problem. If there are needs of identity to be satisfied, if the pursuit of these needs is frustrated, and if once frustrated there are uncontrollable emotional responses, then no policies are going to prevent crime and violence, even though some may curb and help to control them. Problems must be dealt with at their sources.

Putting behaviour back into political analysis makes it possible to articulate the basic approaches that are derived from the human needs and problem-solving frame. Different cultures and political systems, at different stages of development, will have different policies. The primary goal is to provide a role for all members of society, thus avoiding alienation and exclusion. Doles and other social security measures do not do this. Food and shelter alone do not provide an answer to the alienation problem. Where rewarding jobs are not available, other means of identity must be found.

The 20 per cent problem calls for, by one means or another, universal coverage, at levels to be determined in given circumstances, of education and apprenticeship training; health care; job opportunities, paid or voluntary, or other means of identity; workers' compensation for injury; and pensions. The means of accomplishing this are the debating issue, especially in a power political system. The direct way is to have a comprehensive strategy which ensures a role in society for all its members: a modification of the dreaded welfare state system. There is an infinite number of jobs that could be available bearing in mind educational needs, environmental challenges, regeneration of resources, caring, etc. This is the issue that still has to be fought through on an analytical and costing basis.

Trying to deal with civilizations in crisis by changes in interest rates, by reducing income tax in the hope of promoting investment, by punitive policies, while neglecting core problems such as child development, will be seen in retrospect as a major disaster. The main role of public authorities, especially in the corporate state as it is now emerging, is to ensure care of child development at all stages through to finding a first job, and from then on to ensure a sense of role and security in society. Societies cannot afford for any person to perceive himself or herself as being excluded from the social system.

Policies that promote socially acceptable means of satisfying human needs logically substitute the goal of quality of life for economic well-being. By this is meant, essentially, that they would place a high value on individual identity, traditionally neglected.

Conflict resolution

The empirical evidence has been that peace-keeping and like attempts to prevent conflict are self-defeating. But unlike the 1960s and 1970s, when power politics and strategic studies dominated the study of International Relations, there are now theoretical explanations as to why deterrence does not deter and there are alternatives to deterrence strategies. There are known and tested means by which parties can be helped to be analytical about their conflicts so that there can be accurate costing of the consequences of their policies. These need to be pursued in respect of particular conflicts.

In a global setting in which conflict is almost universal, resolving or avoiding a particular conflict is still of significance. But even more important globally and in the longer term is the pursuit of policies that anticipate and avoid conflict. It is analytical and costing processes that are most likely to change perceptions of conflict and shift parties away from threat and deterrence strategies towards avoidance policies.

The two, resolution and avoidance, are in practice related. The insights that are gained from facilitated conflict resolution processes give clues to the hidden causes of conflict and, by deduction, to positive policies. It is this kind of facilitated interactive experience and the accurate costing of consequences of policies that could lead parties to disputes to implement those changes that are required to avoid cold and hot wars.

The behavioural component

We come back to the observation made by Tillich previously quoted. 'A socially defined utopia loses its truth if it does not at the same time fulfil the person, just as the individually defined utopia loses its truth if it does not at the same time bring fulfilment to society.'[8] What has been the persistent characteristic of past and modern societies has been the neglect of the person in the struggle to preserve institutions established to serve the interests of the power elite, whether this be a democratic government, a communist government or a military regime. So much has this been the case that we do not have a language by which to communicate the nature of the problems civilizations face. We have invented a language that seems deliberately to camouflage the divisive issues of our time.

In his book *Consent and Consensus*, P. H. Partridge lists many different meanings of consent which in fact imply an absence of consent.[9] For example, acquiescence for fear of some reprisal is interpreted as consent. There is acquiescence through tradition and propaganda and through apathy. Indeed, the system of elected governments carries the implication that consent has been given for whatever that government chooses to do.

When we look more carefully at decision-making processes the deceptions are even more fundamental. Democracy itself suggests participation and consent. In practice any direct participation and consent there might be is limited to the small percentage of the total population that voted for the elected party. The justification of a parliamentary democracy is that its decisions reflect a consensus, and by implication consensus equals consent. 'Compliance' with consensus norms is required even in the absence of any consent. While consensus refers to the majority opinion of a community, consent implies a personal attitude. Whether there is or can be consent frequently cannot be determined empirically; but it can be deduced from a behavioural analysis. A decision-maker, working within a behavioural frame rather than a power one, could anticipate the reaction of youth to a requirement to conform with a lack of identity, or the reaction of routine workers who are treated as machines.

What we have tried to do in this analysis is to focus on this continuing traditional utopia which is based on the claim that there are those who can expect obedience and those who have a duty to obey. We have argued that if institutions had a behavioural and problem-solving orientation, rather than an exclusive interest-based adversarial one, and were constantly changing to adapt to altering conditions, policies would adapt better to tackling the problems that face civilizations.

The precise nature of institutions and policies must depend on the changing environmental circumstances in which they are determined. By re-examining institutions within a human needs frame we can at least deduce the policy principles that need to be observed. Whether those in a position to make change do so or not will depend finally on how they cost the consequences of maintaining the *status quo* and their interests in preserving the present.

In Part Two we surveyed the kind of change that is required and may be possible in existing adversarial decision-making institutions. But the problem is much deeper. As a result of thousands of years of adversarial experience, humans and human societies have a deeply ingrained culture of adversarial relations. Sports, entertainment, individual status, histories that are taught to the young, all have this combative orientation. From the day a child is born he or she is subject to compulsory compliance, frequently violently enforced. It is an inherited experience transferred in the same way to the next generation. Only in one or two countries is there any required parental training in child-rearing.

We have stressed three areas in which initiatives are likely to be taken by those who have done their costing and have an interest in the future. They include problem-solving decision-making processes at all levels from the family, through the school, to industry and to politics with an emphasis on continuing reassessment of existing institutions and practices; an input into education at all levels that stresses the nature of problem-solving decision-making and the human needs factor in relationships and especially the development of a profession of skilled facilitators; and a far greater emphasis on community action to deal with social problems. There is a growing literature in each of these fields, and a growing interest. But resistances are also growing. There is a need for constantly restating what are the sources of our social and political problems, and the options that are available, and one way of doing this is through appropriate initiatives at all social levels.

As stated at the outset the aim of this book has been to stimulate thinking. If there appears to have been a degree of idiosyncrasy and wishful thinking, this must be taken as part of the stimulation process.

Notes

1   J. Galbraith, *The Culture of Contentment* (Boston, Houghton Mifflin Co., 1992).
2   P. Knightley, 'Goodbye to Great Britain', *The Australian Magazine* (2 April 1994).
3   D. Prothrow-Smith with M. Weissman, *Deadly Consequences: How Violence is Destroying Our Teenage Population and a Plan to Begin Solving the Problem* (New York, Harper Perennial, 1991).

4   Amnesty International, Annual Report (1994).
5   Prothrow-Smith with Weissman, *Deadly Consequences*.
6   New York City Board of Education Report, July 1994.
7   Prothrow-Smith with Weissman, *Deadly Consequences*.
8   P. Tillich, 'Critique and Justification of Utopia', in F. E. Manuel, ed., *Utopias and Utopian Thought* (London, Souvenir Press, 1973).
9   P. H. Partridge, *Consent and Consensus* (London, Pall Mall Press Ltd, 1971).

Bibliography

Banks, M., ed. (1984) *Conflict in World Society: A New Perspective on International Relations*. Brighton: Wheatsheaf Books Ltd.

Boyett, J. and Conn, H. (1992) *Workplace 2000: The Revolution Reshaping American Business*. New York: Nal-Dutton, Plume Books.

Brown, B. and Singer, P. (1996) *The Greens*. Melbourne: The Text Publishing Co.

Burgmann, V. (1993) *Power and Protest: Movements of Change in Australian Society*. New York: Allen and Unwin.

Burton, J. (1969) *Conflict and Communication*. London: Macmillan.

Burton, J. (1972) *World Society*. Cambridge: Cambridge University Press.

Burton, J. (1979) *Deviance, Terrorism and War: The Processes of Solving Unsolved Social and Political Problems*. New York: St Martin's Press; London: Macmillan.

Burton, J. (1984) *Global Conflict: The Domestic Sources of International Crisis*. Brighton: Wheatsheaf Books Ltd.

Burton, J. (1990) *Conflict: Resolution and Provention*. New York: St Martin's Press; London: Macmillan.

Burton, J., ed. (1990) *Conflict: Human Needs Theory*. New York: St Martin's Press; London: Macmillan.

Burton, J. (1996) *Conflict Resolution: Its Language and Processes*. Lanham MD: Scarecrow Press.

Burton, J. and Dukes, F., eds (1990) *Conflict: Readings in Management and Resolution*. New York: St Martin's Press; London: Macmillan.

Burton, J. and Dukes, F. (1990) *Conflict: Practices in Management, Settlement and Resolution*. New York: St Martin's Press; London: Macmillan.

Carten, J. (1992) *A Cold Peace: America, Japan, Germany and the Struggle for Supremacy*. New York: Times Books, The Twentieth Century Fund.

Coate, R. and Rosati, J. (1988) *The Power of Human Needs*. Boulder CO: Lynne Reinner Publishers.

Chomsky, N. (1991) *Deterring Democracy*. New York: Hill and Wang.

Chomsky, N. (1993) *Year 501: The Conquest Continues*. Boston: South End Press.

Davies, J. (1963) *Human Nature in Politics: The Dynamics of Political Behavior*. New York: John Wiley.

Dedring, J. (1976) *Recent Advances in Peace and Conflict Research*. London: Sage.

Deutsch, K. (1963) *The Nerves of Government*. New York: Free Press.

Dryzek, J. S. (1990) *Discursive Democracy*. Cambridge: Cambridge University Press.

Dukes, F. (1996) *Resolving Public Conflict: Transforming Community and Governance*. Manchester: Manchester University Press.

Edwards, P. with Pemberton, G. (1992) *Crisis and Commitments*. Sydney: Allen and Unwin.

Etzioni, A. (1993) *The Spirit of Community: Rights, Responsibilities and the Communitarian Agenda*. New York: Crown Publishers.

Frye, N. (1973) 'Varieties of Literary Utopias', in F. E. Manuel, ed., *Utopias and Utopian Thought*. London: Souvenir Press.

Galbraith, J. (1992) *The Culture of Contentment*. Boston: Houghton Mifflin Co.

Galtung, J. (1964) 'A Structural Theory of Aggression', *Journal of Peace Research*, 1.

Gardiner, J. (1990) *On Leadership*. New York: Free Press.

Gelles, R. (1972) *The Violent Home: A Study of Physical Aggression between Husbands and Wives*. Beverly Hills CA: Sage Publications.

Gelles, R. J. and Straus, M. N. (1988) *Intimate Violence*. New York: Simon and Schuster.

Graubard, S. and Holton, G. (1961) *Excellence and Leadership in a Democracy*. New York: Columbia University Press.

Green, P. (1981) *The Pursuit of Inequality*. New York: Pantheon.

Hamburg, D. (1992) *Today's Children: Creating a Future for a Generation in Crisis*. New York: Times Books, Random House.

Jabri, V. (1996) *Discourses on Violence: Conflict Analysis Reconsidered*. Manchester: Manchester University Press.

Jaros, D. (1973) *Socialization to Politics*. Westport CT: Praeger.

Kennedy, P. (1993) *Preparing for the Twenty-First Century*. New York: Harper and Collins.

Knightley, P. (1994) 'Goodbye to Great Britain', *The Australian Magazine*, 2 April.

Kuhn, T. S. (1970) *The Structure of Scientific Revolutions*. Chicago: University of Chicago Press.

Kwitny, J. (1984) *Endless Enemies. The Making of an Unfriendly World*. New York: Congdon and Weed.

Lederer, K., ed. (1980) *Human Needs*. Cambridge MA: Oelgeschlager, Gunn and Hain.

Lloyd, D. (1964) *The Idea of Law*. Harmondsworth: Pelican Original.

Lloyd-Bostock, S. (1979) 'Explaining Compliance with Imposed Law', in S. Burman and B. Harrell Bond, eds, *The Imposition of Law*. New York: Academic Press.

Mansbridge, J. (1980) *Beyond Adversary Democracy*. New York: Basic Books.

Mansbridge, J., ed., (1990) *Beyond Self Interest*. Chicago, University of Chicago Press.

Manuel, F. E., ed. (1973) *Utopias and Utopian Thought*. London: Souvenir Press.

Maslow, A. (1962) *Towards a Psychology of Being*. Princeton NJ: Princeton Press.

Mathews, J. (1989) *Tools of Change*. Sydney: Pluto Press.

Mitchell, C. (1981) *Peacemaking and the Consultant's Role*. Farnborough: Gower; New York: Nicols.

Morgenthau, H. (1948) *Politics Among Nations: The Struggle for Power and Peace*. New York: Knopf.

Mumford, L. (1973) 'Utopia: The City and the Machine', in F. E. Manuel, ed., *Utopias and Utopian Thought*. London: Souvenir Press.

Murphy, J. (1993) *Harvest of Fear: A History of Australia's Vietnam War*. Sydney: Allen and Unwin.

Odder, D., Ostrov, E. and Howard, K. (1981) *The Adolescent*. New York: Basic Books.

Omar, D. (1996) 'And Justice for All', *Track Two* (Rondebosch, Journal of the Centre for Conflict Resolution), 5: 1 (March), pp. 4–6.

Paige, G. (1977) *The Scientific Study of Political Leadership*. New York: Free Press.

Partridge, P. H. (1971) *Consent and Consensus*. London: Pall Mall Press Ltd.

Peirce, C. S. (1992) *The Essentials of Peirce*, ed. N. Houser and C. Kloesel. Bloomington: Indiana University Press.

Pinnock, D. (1996) 'Gangs, Guns and Rites of Passage', *Track Two* (Rondebosch, Journal of the Centre for Conflict Resolution), 5: 1 (March), p. 10.

Plant, J. and C., eds (1992) *Putting Power in its Place: Create Community Control*. Philadelphia PA: New Society Publishers.

Post, J. and Robins, R. (1993) *When Illness Strikes the Leader: The Dilemma of the Captive King*. New Haven CT: Yale University Press.

Postman, N. (1993). *Technopoly: The Surrender of Culture to Technology*. New York: Vintage Press.

Prothrow-Smith, D. with Weissman, M. (1991) *Deadly Consequences: How Violence is Destroying our Teenage Population and a Plan to Begin Solving the Problem*. New York: Harper Perennial.

Reich, R. (1992) *The Work of Nations*. New York: Vintage Press.

Renshon, S. (1974) *Psychological Needs and Political Behavior: A Theory of Personality and Political Efficacy*. New York: Free Press.

Rogers, J. and Streeck, W. (1994) 'Workplace Representation Overseas', in R. Freeman, ed., *Working under Different Rules*. New York: Russell Sage Foundation.

Rothstein, R. (1994) 'The Global Hiring Hall', *The American Prospect* (Spring).

Rubenstein, R. (1987) *Alchemists of Revolution: Terrorism in the Modern World*. New York: Basic Books.

Rubenstein, R. and associates, *Frameworks for Interpreting Conflict: A Handbook for Journalists, Institute for Conflict Analysis and Resolution*. George Mason University, Virginia, Report No. 2.

Rugege, S. (1996) 'Conflict Resolution', *Track Two* (Rondebosch, Journal of the Centre for Conflict Resolution), 5: 1 (March), p. 23.

Sandole, D. and Merwe, H., eds (1993) *Conflict Resolution. Theory and Practice: Integration and Practice*. Manchester: Manchester University Press.

Schlesinger, A. M. (1992) *The Disuniting of America: Reflections on a Multicultural Society*. New York: Norton and Co.

Schwartz, B. (1994) *The Cost of Living: How Market Freedom Erodes the Best Things in Life*. New York: Norton and Co.

Schwartz, D. and S., eds (1975) *New Directions in Political Socialization*. New York: Free Press.

Sites, P. (1973) *Control: The Basis of Social Order*. New York: Dunellen Publishers.

Sites, P. (1990) 'Needs as Analogues of Emotions', in John Burton, ed., *Conflict: Human Needs Theory*. New York: St Martin's Press; London: Macmillan.

Slaby, M. N. and Roedell, W. C. (1982) 'The Development and Regulation of Aggression in Young Children', in J. Worell, ed., *Psychological Development in the Elementary Years*. Columbia MA: Academic Press, Inc.

Stein, P., Richman, J. and Hannon, N. (1977) *The Family: Functions, Conflicts and Symbols*. Menlo Park CA: Addison Wesley.

Tillett, G. (1991) *Resolving Conflict: A Practical Approach*. Sydney: Sydney University Press.

Tillich, P. (1973) 'Critique and Justification of Utopia', in F. E. Manuel, ed., *Utopias and Utopian Thought*. London: Souvenir Press.

West, C. (1993) *Race Matters*. Boston: Beacon Press.

Wiener, N. (1950) *The Human Use of Human Beings*. New York: Eyre and Spottiswoode.

Whimbey, A. and Lockhead, J. (1982) *Problemsolving and Comprehension*. Philadelphia: Franklin Institute Press.

Index

Page references in <u>italics</u> relate to notes